A New

Way to

Bake

A New
Way to
Bake

Classic Recipes Updated
with Better-for-You Ingredients
from the Modern Pantry

From the Kitchens of
Martha Stewart

CLARKSON POTTER/PUBLISHERS
NEW YORK

Published in the United States by
Clarkson Potter/Publishers, an imprint
of the Crown Publishing Group,
a division of Penguin Random House
LLC, New York
crownpublishing.com
marthastewart.com

CLARKSON POTTER is a trademark
and POTTER with colophon is a
registered trademark of Penguin
Random House LLC.

Library of Congress
Cataloging-in-Publication Data
is available upon request.

ISBN 978-0-307-95471-8

eBook ISBN 978-0-307-95472-5

Printed in China

Book and cover design
by Jennifer Wagner

Cover photography
by Jonathan Lovekin

10 9 8 7 6 5 4 3 2 1

First Edition

All Photographs by Jonathan Lovekin,
except the following:
Bryan Gardner (pages 11, 201)
Raymond Hom (pages 28, 167, 176)
Yunhee Kim (page 32)
Johnny Miller (pages 142, 162, 228, 250)
Marcus Nilsson (pages 84, 246, 270, 273)
Con Poulos (pages 30, 92, 148, 191, 202, 210)
Andrew Purcell (page 45)
Alpha Smoot (page 100)
Lennart Weibull (pages 82, 171, 189, 261)
Anna Williams (page 110)
Linda Xiao (pages 129, 130, 133)

Contents

FOREWORD

If you've ever kneaded a soft, fragrant mound of yeast dough, mixed up a batch of biscuits, or crumbled streusel over coffee cake batter, you will understand why I am extolling the virtues of this, our newest cookbook, *A New Way to Bake*. From cover to cover, this book fulfills its promise to provide you with extraordinary recipes and information about alternative ways to bake old favorites. Using a new repertoire of grains, flours, and sweeteners, your muffins, pancakes, cookies, and tarts will taste different, and you, the baker, will learn a whole new vocabulary. Millet and amaranth, buckwheat and spelt, seeds and nuts, among many ingredients, will transform the ordinary into the extraordinary, and your family will experience tastes and textures heretofore unknown.

During the development phase of the recipes in this book, I made a point of visiting the test kitchen on a daily basis to savor and enjoy unusually delicious creations fresh from the ovens. It was impossible to choose my favorites because each and every recipe was unique, flavorful, beautifully complex, and positively wholesome.

For those of you trying to cut back on the use of white flour, you will be pleasantly surprised how other grains can easily take its place, resulting in pleasurable surprises like graham-flour tart crust, spelt blondies, yeasted whole-wheat waffles, or vegan French toast. And the special section devoted to easy cake finishes, chocolate varieties, and glossaries of grains and sweeteners will prove a valuable addition to your cookbook library. Enjoy yourself as you explore this "new way to bake"!

Martha Stewart

BAKING FROM THE MODERN PANTRY

1 Seek out the best ingredients.

Opt for minimally processed whole-grain flours, full-fat milks and yogurts, natural sugars, and organic eggs whenever possible. You can find small-batch, artisan-made items—like freshly milled flours and traditional buttermilk—at farmers' markets and specialty grocers. Likewise, choose locally grown fruits, vegetables, and herbs. Buy whole spices and grind them yourself. Remember that the best ingredients will produce the best-tasting baked goods, every time.

2 Store things well.

Whole-grain flours, nuts, and seeds all contain fat, which makes them prone to rancidity. To extend their shelf life, keep them in resealable plastic bags in a cool, dry place—or better yet, in your freezer or refrigerator. To check for freshness, sniff the ingredient: Grains, nuts, and seeds should smell sweet, never rancid.

3 Make it your own.

With the wider availability of alternative flours, milks, sweeteners, and oils, the rules of baking are constantly being revised and rewritten. Think of these recipes as great jumping-off points; don't be afraid to play around to create something distinctly your own. (Use the chart on page 298 as a guide.) Try swapping in a small amount of one type of flour or sweetener for another, and pay attention to the differences. Keep a record of changes in taste or texture. Start out with small tweaks, then slowly increase or decrease the proportions as you like.

4 Take your time.

Baking should never be rushed, especially when working with many of the ingredients featured in this book. Some whole-grain flours can take longer to hydrate than all-purpose. Pie doughs, which are always chilled before rolling, will benefit from a longer rest when they are made with whole grains than those made with all-purpose flour. It's an optional step, but if you have the time, let muffin and quickbread batters rest for 15 minutes before baking; the results will be more moist and fine-textured. And letting yeasted bread rise slowly overnight allows it to develop a more complex flavor.

5 Keep freshness in mind.

Most recipes indicate how far ahead a recipe can be prepared. Sometimes that means making different components at different times, then combining and assembling just before serving. Follow these suggestions as you bake, so you are sure to present—and enjoy—baked goods when they will taste their very best.

Breakfast

Gluten-Free Quinoa Pancakes

Whole-Wheat Pancakes

Chickpea-Vegetable Pancakes

Vegan Banana-Oat Pancakes

Vegan French Toast

Buckwheat Waffles

Overnight Yeasted Granola
Waffles

Double-Apple Bran Muffins

Blueberry Muffins

Blackberry–Oat Bran Muffins

Cranberry-Almond Muffins

Parsnip-Rosemary Muffins

Corn Muffins

Quinoa Crumb Cakes
with Pecans and Dates

Double-Chocolate Rye Muffins

Sprouted Spelt Banana-Nut
Muffins

Spiced Apple and Oat
Scones

Pumpkin Spelt Scones with
Maple Glaze

Buttermilk Barley Biscuits

Cornmeal Drop Biscuits

Seeded Breakfast Rolls

Whole-Wheat Sticky Buns

Oat-and-Millet Granola

Mixed-Seed Clusters

Breakfast Cookies

Coconut Baked Oatmeal

Swiss Chard and Sausage
Strata

Gluten-Free Quinoa Pancakes

You may not think to use cooked grains in your baked goods, but they're a wonderful way to add substance and fiber and, in the case of quinoa, to boost ~~protein content. Sweetened with just a little maple~~ syrup, these pancakes are ~~...~~ ble-grain goodness, swap in

Regrettably, the recipe for

Gluten-Free Quinoa Pancakes (page 13)

was misprinted. To make the pancakes gluten-free, substitute ¾ cup quinoa flour (or if you prefer, gluten-free all-purpose flour) for the ¾ cup all-purpose flour.

ot, combine quinoa with water and l; cover and simmer over medium-til the quinoa is tender and water is bout 16 minutes. Let cool completely.

n to 200°F. In a bowl, whisk inoa, flour, baking powder, and her bowl, whisk together eggs, r, milk, and syrup until smooth. xture to flour mixture and whisk

t a large nonstick skillet or griddle and heat over medium-high. For ke, drop 2 tablespoons batter into k until bubbles appear on top, Flip cakes and cook until golden ndersides, 2 minutes. Wipe skil-nd repeat with more butter and batter (reduce heat to medium if oo quickly). Keep pancakes warm in ve immediately, with maple syrup rries, if desired.

Whole-Wheat Pancakes

No need to incorporate white flour along with the whole-wheat—these pancakes are as fluffy and as tender as ever. You can make this your go-to Sunday morning recipe; serve with the jammy topping here or whatever you usually like alongside. SERVES 6

For the pancakes

1¼ cups whole-wheat flour

¼ cup toasted wheat germ

2 tablespoons natural cane sugar

1½ teaspoons baking powder

½ teaspoon baking soda

1 teaspoon coarse salt

1½ cups buttermilk

¼ cup safflower oil or melted coconut oil, plus more for pan

2 large eggs, lightly beaten

Water, if necessary

For the compote

1 pint fresh blueberries (2 cups)

¼ cup plus 2 tablespoons fresh lemon juice

⅛ teaspoon coarse salt

½ cup natural cane sugar

½ pint fresh blackberries (1 cup)

Make the pancakes: Preheat oven to 200°F. In a bowl, whisk together flour, wheat germ, sugar, baking powder, baking soda, and salt. Whisk in buttermilk, oil, and eggs. Let stand 10 minutes (if batter thickens too much, stir in 1 tablespoon water).

Make the compote: In a saucepan, heat blueberries, lemon juice, and salt over medium heat, stirring, until berries begin to burst, 4 to 5 minutes. Stir in sugar. Simmer, stirring often, until thick enough to coat the back of a spoon, 6 to 8 minutes. Transfer to a bowl and stir in blackberries.

Lightly coat a large nonstick skillet or griddle with oil, and heat over medium. Spoon in 2 tablespoons batter for each pancake. Cook until bubbles appear, about 2 minutes; flip, and cook until golden brown, about 2 minutes. Keep pancakes warm in oven or serve immediately with compote.

Chickpea-Vegetable Pancakes

Thicker than Mediterranean-style chickpea-flour flatbreads, these gluten-free pancakes take their flavor cues from the American Southwest. Mixed with peppers, scallions, and carrots in the batter, and topped with yogurt and avocado, they're a great savory breakfast option. SERVES 4

1¼ cups chickpea flour

¾ teaspoon coarse salt

¼ teaspoon baking powder

¼ teaspoon ground cumin

½ cup water

½ red or yellow bell pepper, finely diced

2 scallions, thinly sliced, plus more for serving

2 carrots, peeled and coarsely grated

2 tablespoons extra-virgin olive oil

½ cup Greek yogurt, for serving

1 ripe avocado, diced, for serving

Preheat oven to 200°F. In a bowl, whisk together chickpea flour, salt, baking powder, and cumin. Add water and stir until combined. (Batter should be thick.) Fold in diced pepper, scallions, and carrots.

In a skillet, heat oil over medium. For each pancake, drop ¼ cup batter into skillet and cook until browned, 3 to 4 minutes per side. Keep warm in oven while you cook remaining pancakes. Serve with yogurt, avocado, and scallions.

Vegan Banana-Oat Pancakes

In these pancakes, almond milk and coconut oil stand in for dairy (milk and butter), while oat flour (which you can make by grinding rolled oats in the food processor) and unsweetened coconut replace any wheat flour. Flaxseed meal, which becomes gel-like when moistened, provides the structure and thickening power an egg otherwise would, and mashed banana and orange juice sweeten these naturally. The result is a delicious vegan, wheat-free breakfast. SERVES 2

½ mashed ripe banana

½ cup unsweetened almond milk

3 tablespoons flaxseed meal (ground flaxseeds)

4 teaspoons virgin coconut oil, melted

½ cup oat flour

½ cup unsweetened shredded coconut

¼ cup fresh orange juice

½ teaspoon baking powder

½ teaspoon ground cinnamon

Pinch coarse salt

1 clementine, peel and pith removed, segmented

Honey, for serving

Preheat oven to 200°F. In a bowl, mix banana, almond milk, flaxseed meal, and 2 teaspoons coconut oil; let stand until thick, about 10 minutes.

Whisk in oat flour, shredded coconut, orange juice, baking powder, cinnamon, and salt.

Heat remaining 2 teaspoons coconut oil in a cast-iron skillet over medium. Working in batches, spoon in ¼ cup batter and flatten into 3-inch rounds with a spatula. Cook until golden, flipping once, about 6 minutes per side. Keep warm in oven while you cook remaining pancakes. Serve with orange segments and honey.

Vegan French Toast

Tofu, mashed bananas, and almond milk create the "custard" for this surprisingly luscious egg- and dairy-free French toast. The recipe works best with day-old bread. If using a fresh baguette, let it soak in the custard for half the soaking time; otherwise, it could fall apart. SERVES 6

---

1 small banana, plus 1 more sliced (for serving)

6 ounces silken tofu (¾ cup)

3 tablespoons pure maple syrup, plus more for serving

1 cup unsweetened almond milk

1 teaspoon vanilla extract

1 teaspoon ground cinnamon

¼ teaspoon coarse salt

1 baguette, preferably day-old, cut on a bias into 1-inch-thick slices

2 to 3 tablespoons safflower oil or virgin coconut oil

Fresh raspberries, for serving

Confectioners' sugar, for dusting (optional)

Preheat oven to 200°F. In a blender or food processor, puree whole banana, tofu, maple syrup, almond milk, vanilla, cinnamon, and salt until smooth. Transfer to a large, shallow dish.

Working in batches, soak bread in banana mixture, 3 to 4 minutes per side. In a nonstick skillet, heat 1 tablespoon oil over medium. Lift bread from banana mixture, allowing excess to drip off, and transfer to skillet.

Cook bread, flipping once, until a golden crust forms, 5 to 6 minutes per side. Keep warm in oven while cooking remaining batches, adding more oil as necessary. Serve French toast topped with bananas, raspberries, and maple syrup. Dust with confectioners' sugar, if desired.

Buckwheat Waffles

One way to wake up to a brighter morning: Top lightly sweetened waffles with colorful fruit. We like to use three varieties of sunny citrus in winter and fresh berries in summer. The earthy buckwheat flour here is perfect with the milky ricotta. MAKES ABOUT 6

For the waffles

- 1 cup buckwheat flour
- 1 cup all-purpose flour
- ¼ cup natural cane sugar
- 1½ teaspoons baking powder
- ½ teaspoon coarse salt
- 1½ cups milk
- 4 tablespoons unsalted butter, melted and cooled
- 1 large egg
- Oil, for brushing, as needed

For the topping

- 1½ cups fresh ricotta
- 2 blood oranges, peel and pith removed, sliced or segmented
- 2 Cara Cara oranges, peel and pith removed, sliced or segmented (see note)
- 4 clementines, peel and pith removed, sliced or segmented
- Honey or pure maple syrup, for serving

Make the waffles: In a bowl, whisk together both flours, sugar, baking powder, and salt. In another bowl, whisk together milk, butter, and egg until combined. Stir milk mixture into flour mixture until just combined. Let batter stand, uncovered, for 20 minutes.

Preheat oven to 200°F. Preheat a waffle iron and lightly oil as necessary. Place about ½ cup batter (depending on your iron) in the center of the iron, and spread gently. Cook according to manufacturer's instructions, 5 to 8 minutes. Keep warm in oven while you cook the remaining waffles. (Waffles can be frozen in a single layer on a baking sheet and stored in a resealable plastic bag up to 1 month. Reheat in a 300°F oven or toaster oven.)

Top the waffles: Spoon ricotta over waffles and top with citrus fruits. Drizzle with honey or syrup, and serve.

To peel citrus use a sharp chef's knife: Stand the fruit up on a work surface, and slice to remove all the pith following the shape of the fruit. To create segments, cut in between the membranes to release the fruit.

Overnight Yeasted Granola Waffles

Here's an excellent reason to plan breakfast in advance: These yeasted whole-wheat waffles rise overnight, which gives them time to develop an incredibly complex flavor. Sprinkling granola over the batter just before each waffle is cooked adds extra sweetness and crunch. You can use homemade granola (page 63) or any store-bought variety without dried fruit. MAKES 6

½ cup warm water (about 110°F)

1 envelope (¼ ounce) active dry yeast (2¼ teaspoons)

1 stick (½ cup) unsalted butter, melted

2 cups milk

¼ cup plus 2 tablespoons natural cane sugar

1½ cups all-purpose flour

1½ cups whole-wheat flour

1 teaspoon coarse salt

Oil, for brushing, as needed

2 large eggs, lightly beaten

½ teaspoon baking soda

1½ cups granola (without dried fruit)

Pure maple syrup, for serving

In a large bowl, combine the water, yeast, melted butter, milk, and sugar; let stand about 5 minutes. Stir in both flours and salt. Cover with plastic, and let stand at room temperature overnight. (The batter will double in bulk and deflate.)

Preheat a waffle iron and lightly oil as necessary. Stir eggs and baking soda into batter. Place about ½ cup of batter (depending on your iron) in the center of the iron, and spread gently. Sprinkle with 3 to 4 tablespoons granola. Cook according to manufacturer's instructions, 5 to 8 minutes. Keep warm in oven or serve immediately, with maple syrup. (Waffles can be frozen in a single layer on a baking sheet and stored in a resealable plastic bag up to 1 month. Reheat in a 300°F oven or toaster oven.)

Double-Apple Bran Muffins

Apples pull double duty in these not-too-sweet bran muffins, made with half all-purpose flour and half wheat bran. Applesauce makes them especially moist, and diced apple creates bursts of fruity sweetness. The real surprise here is millet, which is added whole and uncooked for some healthy crunch.

MAKES 1 DOZEN

- 1 cup all-purpose flour
- 1 cup wheat bran or toasted wheat germ
- 2 tablespoons millet (see note)
- 1 teaspoon baking soda
- ½ teaspoon coarse salt
- 1 stick (½ cup) unsalted butter, melted and slightly cooled
- ¼ cup plus 2 tablespoons packed light brown sugar
- 1 large egg
- 1 cup unsweetened applesauce
- 1 small Granny Smith apple, peeled, cored, and cut into ¼-inch pieces (about 1 cup)

Preheat oven to 350°F. Line a 12-cup muffin tin with paper liners. In a bowl, whisk together flour, wheat bran, millet, baking soda, and salt. In another bowl, whisk together butter, brown sugar, egg, and applesauce until well combined. Stir butter mixture into flour mixture, until just combined. Fold in apple.

Divide batter evenly among muffin cups. Bake, rotating pan halfway through, just until muffin tops spring back when lightly touched and a cake tester inserted into centers of the muffins comes out clean, about 24 minutes. Let cool in pan on a wire rack 5 minutes, then transfer muffins to rack and let cool completely. (Muffins can be kept in an airtight container at room temperature up to 2 days.)

Now that you have an open bag of millet, what do you do with it? Add a few tablespoons of uncooked millet to other batters and doughs (like the Breakfast Cookies on page 67). Or serve cooked millet with toppings for a warm breakfast or as a side dish for dinner.

Blueberry Muffins

An otherwise classic blueberry muffin gets a healthy makeover with whole-wheat flour and wheat germ. Sweetened with brown sugar, it also has a richer flavor than those made with granulated sugar. A streusel-like mixture of oats, more wheat germ, and light brown sugar sprinkled on top turns golden and crisp in the oven. MAKES 1 DOZEN

For the muffins

- ¾ cup whole-wheat flour
- ¾ cup all-purpose flour
- ½ cup toasted wheat germ
- 2 teaspoons baking powder
- ¼ teaspoon coarse salt
- ⅔ cup packed light brown sugar
- ¾ cup milk
- ¼ cup safflower oil
- 2 large eggs, lightly beaten
- 1 teaspoon vanilla extract
- 1½ cups blueberries

For the topping

- ¼ cup old-fashioned rolled oats
- 2 tablespoons toasted wheat germ
- 1 tablespoon packed light brown sugar

Make the muffins: Preheat oven to 375°F. Line a 12-cup muffin tin with paper liners. In a bowl, whisk together both flours, wheat germ, baking powder, salt, and brown sugar.

Make a well in center of bowl and add milk, oil, eggs, and vanilla. Gently mix until just combined. Fold in blueberries. Divide batter evenly among muffin cups.

Make the topping: In a small bowl, combine oats, wheat germ, and sugar. Sprinkle evenly over batter.

Bake, rotating pan halfway through, until a cake tester inserted into centers of muffins comes out clean, 20 to 22 minutes. Let cool in pan on a wire rack 5 minutes, then transfer muffins to rack and let cool completely. (Muffins can be kept in an airtight container at room temperature up to 2 days.)

Blackberry-Oat Bran Muffins

Oat bran adds lots of fiber to these cakey muffins, and the natural flavor of oats is a great pairing for the berries. If you can't find oat bran, you can substitute wheat bran. MAKES 1 DOZEN

1½ cups all-purpose flour

⅔ cup oat bran

2 teaspoons baking powder

½ teaspoon baking soda

½ teaspoon ground cinnamon

¼ teaspoon coarse salt

6 tablespoons unsalted butter, room temperature

½ cup plus 1 tablespoon natural cane sugar

2 large eggs

2 teaspoons vanilla extract

1 cup buttermilk

1½ cups blackberries, chopped if large

Preheat oven to 375°F. Line a 12-cup muffin tin with paper liners. In a bowl, whisk together flour, oat bran, baking powder, baking soda, cinnamon, and salt.

In a large bowl, with an electric mixer, beat butter and ½ cup sugar on high until pale and fluffy, about 2 minutes. Beat in eggs and vanilla until combined. With mixer on low, add flour mixture in two additions, alternating with buttermilk, and beat until combined. Fold in blackberries.

Divide batter evenly among muffin cups and sprinkle with remaining 1 tablespoon sugar. Bake, rotating pan halfway through, until a cake tester inserted into centers of muffins comes out with moist crumbs attached, 20 to 25 minutes. Let cool in pan on a wire rack 5 minutes, then transfer muffins to rack and let cool completely. (Muffins can be kept in an airtight container at room temperature up to 2 days.)

Cranberry-Almond Muffins

We love that these tart berries are available fresh in the market when locally grown summer berries are out of season. Plus, the orange zest used in the muffins is a classic pairing with cranberries, and both ingredients are delicious with the heartier almond and whole-wheat flours here. MAKES 16

1¼ cups plus 1 tablespoon natural cane sugar

1 cup whole-wheat flour

¾ cup all-purpose flour

¼ cup almond flour

1 teaspoon baking soda

¼ teaspoon coarse salt

⅔ cup milk

⅔ cup plain yogurt

2 large eggs

1 teaspoon finely grated orange zest plus ¼ cup fresh orange juice (from 1 navel orange)

1 cup fresh or thawed frozen cranberries

½ cup sliced almonds

Preheat oven to 350°F. Line 16 cups of two 12-cup muffin tins with paper liners.

In a large bowl, whisk together 1¼ cups sugar, all flours, baking soda, and salt. In another bowl, whisk together milk, yogurt, eggs, and orange zest and juice. Fold milk mixture into flour mixture; then gently fold in cranberries until just combined.

Divide batter evenly among muffin cups, and sprinkle with remaining 1 tablespoon sugar and the almonds. Bake, rotating pans halfway through, until a cake tester inserted into center of muffins comes out clean, about 20 minutes. Let cool in pan on a wire rack 5 minutes, then transfer muffins to rack and let cool completely. (Muffins can be kept in an airtight container at room temperature up to 2 days.)

Parsnip-Rosemary Muffins

Parsnips add earthy sweetness and moisture to baked goods, like their close cousins, carrots. Because these whole-wheat muffins lean toward savory, you can serve them for breakfast or at lunch or dinner, with soup. If you'd rather make a strictly sweet muffin, swap in one-quarter teaspoon cinnamon for the rosemary and sprinkle the tops with sugar instead of salt. MAKES 1 DOZEN

---

1 cup all-purpose flour

¾ cup whole-wheat flour

¾ cup natural cane sugar

2½ teaspoons baking powder

½ teaspoon coarse salt

1 cup plain yogurt

¼ cup safflower oil

2 large eggs, plus 2 large egg whites

1 cup grated parsnip (from 2 medium peeled parsnips)

¾ teaspoon chopped fresh rosemary, plus whole rosemary leaves, for garnish

Flaky salt, for sprinkling

Preheat oven to 350°F. Line a 12-cup muffin tin with paper liners.

In a bowl, whisk together both flours, sugar, baking powder, and salt. In another bowl, whisk together yogurt, oil, eggs, and egg whites. Fold yogurt mixture into flour mixture; then gently fold in parsnips and chopped rosemary until just combined.

Divide batter evenly among muffin cups, and sprinkle each with a pinch of flaky salt and a few whole rosemary leaves. Bake, rotating pan halfway through, until a cake tester inserted into centers of the muffins comes out clean, about 25 minutes. Let cool in pan on a wire rack, 5 minutes, then transfer muffins to rack and let cool completely. (Muffins can be kept in an airtight container at room temperature up to 2 days.)

Corn Muffins

Cornmeal is naturally flavorful and gluten-free but won't produce the lightness you want for muffins if you use it on its own. All-purpose flour gives this muffin lift and structure. Grapes are an unexpected addition. If you prefer, you can swap in blueberries or raspberries or make the muffin savory, folding in one cup of grated cheddar cheese and omitting the sugar that's sprinkled on top. MAKES 1 DOZEN

---

1 cup plus 2 tablespoons yellow cornmeal

1 cup all-purpose flour

⅔ cup plus 1 tablespoon natural cane sugar

1 tablespoon baking powder

1¼ teaspoons coarse salt

¼ cup safflower oil

4 tablespoons unsalted butter, melted

2 tablespoons honey

2 large eggs, lightly beaten

1 cup milk

1½ cups seedless red grapes, halved (optional)

Preheat oven to 375°F. Line a 12-cup muffin tin with paper liners. In a bowl, whisk together cornmeal, flour, ⅔ cup sugar, baking powder, and salt. In another bowl, whisk together oil, butter, honey, eggs, and milk. Fold oil mixture into cornmeal mixture; then gently fold in 1 cup grapes, if desired, until just combined.

Divide batter evenly among muffin cups. Top with remaining ½ cup grapes, if desired, and sprinkle with remaining tablespoon sugar. Bake until a cake tester inserted into centers of muffins comes out clean, about 20 minutes. Let cool in pan on a rack. (Muffins can be kept in an airtight container at room temperature up to 2 days.)

Quinoa Crumb Cakes with Pecans and Dates

Everyone loves a streusel-topped crumb cake for breakfast—or any time of day, really. This one includes bright notes of orange zest, crunchy pecans, and an interesting mix of flours, including spelt and quinoa. MAKES 18

For the crumb topping

- ¾ cup spelt flour
- ¼ cup plus 2 tablespoons packed light brown sugar
- 3 tablespoons natural cane sugar
- ⅛ teaspoon coarse salt
- ⅛ teaspoon ground cinnamon
- 6 tablespoons cold unsalted butter, cut into pieces

For the cakes

- 2 sticks (1 cup) unsalted butter, room temperature, plus more for pans
- 1 cup all-purpose flour
- 1 cup quinoa flour
- 2 teaspoons baking powder
- 1 teaspoon coarse salt
- 1 cup packed light brown sugar
- 2 large eggs
- 1½ teaspoons vanilla extract
- 1 teaspoon finely grated orange zest
- 1 cup buttermilk
- ¾ cup coarsely chopped pecans, toasted (see page 288)
- 1 cup coarsely chopped dried dates (about 14)

Make the crumb topping: In a bowl, whisk together flour, both sugars, salt, and cinnamon. Cut in butter using a pastry blender or rub in with your fingers until small to medium clumps form. Freeze while you prepare cakes.

Make the cakes: Preheat oven to 350°F. Butter 18 cups of two 12-cup muffin tins. In a bowl, whisk together both flours, baking powder, and salt.

In another bowl, with an electric mixer, beat butter and brown sugar on medium-high until pale and fluffy, about 3 minutes. Add eggs, one at a time, beating until just combined. Add vanilla and orange zest. With mixer on low, add flour mixture, alternating with buttermilk, in three additions, beginning and ending with flour. Fold in chopped pecans and dates.

Divide batter evenly among prepared muffin cups, and sprinkle tops of each with crumb topping. Bake, rotating pans halfway through, until cakes are golden brown and spring back to the touch, and a cake tester inserted in centers of the cakes comes out with a few moist crumbs, 22 to 25 minutes. Let cool in pan on a wire rack 5 minutes, then transfer cakes to rack and let cool completely. (Cakes can be kept in an airtight container at room temperature up to 2 days.)

Double-Chocolate Rye Muffins

What's not to love about chocolate for breakfast? Free of all-purpose flour, these muffins rely on a mix of rye and spelt flours, adding malty flavors reminiscent of chocolate stout. Dark rye flour includes more of the grain's bran layer and makes the muffins more hearty and dense; for a lighter texture use light rye flour. MAKES 20

1 cup rye flour

1 cup spelt flour

¼ cup unsweetened Dutch-process cocoa powder

1 teaspoon baking powder

½ teaspoon baking soda

½ teaspoon coarse salt

3 large eggs

⅓ cup packed light brown sugar

1 cup milk

⅔ cup pure maple syrup

1 stick (½ cup) plus 2 tablespoons unsalted butter, melted and cooled

4 ounces bittersweet chocolate, coarsely chopped

Preheat oven to 350°F. Line 20 cups of two 12-cup muffin tins with paper liners.

In a bowl, whisk together both flours, cocoa powder, baking powder, baking soda, and salt.

In another bowl, whisk eggs and brown sugar until foamy, about 1 minute. Whisk in milk, maple syrup, and melted butter. Carefully fold in flour mixture just until combined (do not overmix). Fold in half the chopped chocolate.

Divide batter evenly among prepared muffin cups, and top with remaining chopped chocolate. Bake, rotating pans halfway through, until muffins spring back to touch and a cake tester inserted into centers of muffins comes out with moist crumbs, about 18 minutes. Let cool in pan on a wire rack 5 minutes, then transfer muffins to rack and let cool completely. (Muffins can be kept in an airtight container at room temperature up to 2 days.)

Sprouted Spelt Banana-Nut Muffins

When combined with bananas, walnuts, and butter, spelt flour brings toasty butterscotch flavor to maple-sweetened muffins. Sprouted flour, made from sprouted grains, tends to be less absorbent than regular flours because the sprouting process converts some of the starch into vegetable sugars. The result? Exceptionally tender muffins. MAKES 1 DOZEN

---

2 cups sprouted spelt flour

2¼ teaspoons baking powder

1 teaspoon coarse salt

¼ teaspoon ground cinnamon

3 extra-ripe bananas, mashed (1 cup)

½ cup packed light brown sugar

¼ cup pure maple syrup

1 large egg

1 stick (½ cup) unsalted butter, melted and cooled

¼ cup milk

1½ cups (5 ounces) walnuts, toasted and coarsely chopped (see page 288)

Raw sugar, such as turbinado, for sprinkling

Preheat oven to 350°F. Line a 12-cup muffin tin with paper liners.

In a bowl, whisk together flour, baking powder, salt, and cinnamon. In another bowl, whisk together bananas, brown sugar, syrup, egg, melted butter, and milk until just combined. Fold banana mixture into flour mixture, then fold in 1 cup chopped walnuts.

Divide batter evenly among prepared cups. Sprinkle with remaining walnuts and turbinado sugar, if desired. Bake, rotating pan halfway through, until tops spring back when lightly touched and a cake tester inserted in centers of the muffins comes out clean, 20 to 22 minutes. Let cool in pan on a wire rack 5 minutes, then transfer muffins to rack and let cool completely. (Muffins can be kept in an airtight container at room temperature up to 2 days.)

Don't be tempted to substitute regular spelt flour for sprouted; the flavor and texture would not be the same.

Spiced Apple and Oat Scones

These Scottish-style scones feature an almost equal proportion of flour and oats. Diced apple and buttermilk keep them tender. (You can substitute spelt flour for the all-purpose.) Cutting them into squares means no scraps. MAKES 12 SCONES

1⅔ cups all-purpose flour, plus more for dusting

1⅓ cups old-fashioned rolled oats, plus more for topping

¼ cup plus 2 tablespoons packed light brown sugar

½ teaspoon ground cinnamon

½ teaspoon freshly grated nutmeg

2 teaspoons baking powder

¾ teaspoon baking soda

½ teaspoon coarse salt

1½ sticks (¾ cup) cold unsalted butter, cut into pieces

1½ cups diced Granny Smith apples (2 apples cut into generous ¼-inch cubes)

⅔ cup cold buttermilk, plus more for brushing

Raw sugar, such as turbinado, for sprinkling

Preheat oven to 400°F. In a bowl, whisk together flour, oats, brown sugar, cinnamon, nutmeg, baking powder, baking soda, and salt. Cut in butter with a pastry blender or rub in with your fingers. (The largest pieces should be the size of small peas.) Using your fingertips, flatten butter pieces into small disks. Stir in apples and buttermilk until dough just comes together.

Turn out dough onto a lightly floured work surface. Pat dough into a 8-by-6-inch rectangle, and cut into twelve 2-inch squares using a floured knife or bench scraper. Place about 2 inches apart on parchment-lined baking sheets. Brush tops with buttermilk, and sprinkle with turbinado sugar and oats.

Bake, rotating sheets halfway through, until golden brown, 20 to 22 minutes. Let cool on sheets for 15 minutes. Serve warm or at room temperature. (Scones are best the day they're made but can be kept in a single layer in an airtight container up to 1 day.)

Pumpkin Spelt Scones with Maple Glaze

Spelt flour is an excellent choice for these autumnal coffee-shop–style scones because it naturally pairs with the same spices as used in pumpkin pie. Plus, it's a lighter flour than whole-wheat, so it can completely replace all-purpose flour here without making the scones dense. Frozen, grated butter needs only to be stirred, rather than cut into the flour, resulting in extra tender scones.

MAKES 8 SCONES

---

2 cups spelt flour

⅓ cup natural cane sugar

2 teaspoons baking powder

¾ teaspoon ground ginger

¾ teaspoon ground cinnamon

½ teaspoon freshly grated nutmeg

Coarse salt

1 stick (½ cup) frozen unsalted butter, grated on large holes of a box grater; plus 1 tablespoon, melted

2 tablespoons heavy cream, plus more for brushing

1 large egg, room temperature

⅓ cup canned unsweetened pumpkin puree

½ cup confectioners' sugar

2 to 3 tablespoons pure maple syrup

Preheat oven to 375°F. In a bowl, whisk together flour, cane sugar, baking powder, ginger, cinnamon, nutmeg, and ¾ teaspoon salt. Stir in grated butter.

In another bowl, whisk together cream, egg, and pumpkin; stir into flour mixture just until a dough forms. (It will still be crumbly.) Pat into a 6-inch round on a parchment-lined baking sheet. Brush with cream. Using a knife or bench scraper, cut dough into 8 wedges, and pull 2 inches apart.

Bake, rotating sheet halfway through, until scones are golden brown, about 20 minutes. Let cool completely on sheet on a wire rack.

In a small bowl, stir together melted butter, confectioners' sugar, 2 tablespoons maple syrup, and a pinch of salt until smooth. If glaze is too thick, add additional maple syrup, 1 teaspoon at a time. Dip tops of scones in glaze and transfer to rack set on baking sheet. Allow glaze to set for 30 minutes before serving. (Scones are best the day they're made but can be kept in a single layer in an airtight container up to 1 day.)

Buttermilk Barley Biscuits

The best biscuits are often made with fine low-protein wheat flours, such as White Lily brand. Whole-grain barley flour is also quite fine and low in gluten, so it creates a lovely, light biscuit that's a bit more wholesome than a biscuit made purely from all-purpose flour (we combine them in equal parts). The dough here gets folded over itself two times (see next page), creating layers of butter that help the biscuits rise high in the oven and become extra flaky. MAKES 9 BISCUITS

2   cups all-purpose flour, plus more for dusting

2   cups barley flour

1   tablespoon plus 1 teaspoon baking powder

¼   teaspoon baking soda

2   tablespoons natural cane sugar

2   teaspoons coarse salt

2   sticks (1 cup) cold unsalted butter, cut into bits; plus 3 tablespoons, melted

1½ cups cold buttermilk

Preheat oven to 450°F. In a food processor, pulse both flours, baking powder, baking soda, sugar, and salt until just combined. Add cold butter; pulse just until mixture is the texture of coarse meal, with a few pea-size pieces of butter remaining. Add buttermilk. Pulse just until dough is moistened, 3 to 4 times (do not overmix).

Turn out dough onto a lightly floured surface and pat into an 8-inch square (see next page for how-to). Fold dough in half and use your hands to shape into a square again. Fold in half and shape into an 8-inch square, about 1 inch thick. Using a sharp knife, trim about ⅛ inch of dough from each side, then cut into 9 equal squares.

Transfer biscuits to a parchment-lined baking sheet, spacing about 2 inches apart. Bake, rotating sheet halfway through, until biscuits are golden, 17 to 18 minutes. Brush tops with melted butter. Serve warm or at room temperature. (Biscuits are best the day they're made but can be kept in a single layer in an airtight container up to 1 day.)

How to Make Layered Biscuits

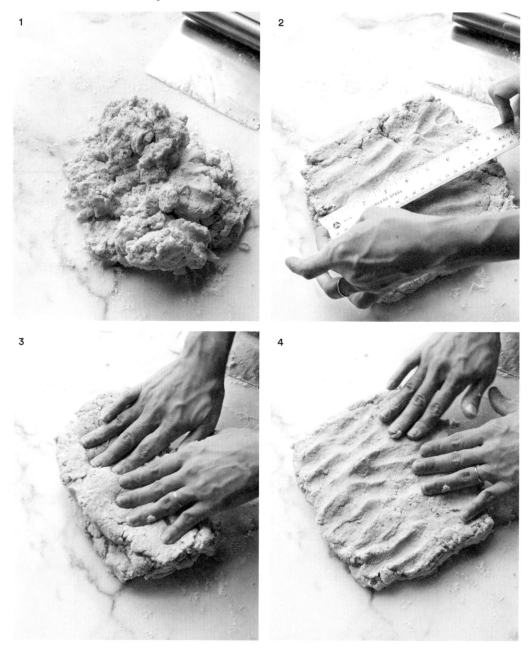

1 Turn out dough onto a lightly floured surface.　**2** Pat dough into an 8-inch square.　**3** Fold dough in half.
4 Shape folded dough into a square; repeat folding and patting one more time to form an 8-inch square.

<u>5</u> Trim off edges (about ⅛ inch from each side) of dough.   <u>6</u> With a sharp knife, cut dough into 9 squares.
<u>7</u> Place squares 2 inches apart on a parchment-lined baking sheet.   <u>8</u> Immediately after baking, brush biscuits evenly with melted butter.

Cornmeal Drop Biscuits

Using finely ground cornmeal makes these biscuits more airy and delicate than those made with coarser ground meal; if you prefer a rustic texture, you can substitute medium grind. Serve the biscuits for breakfast with jam and butter, or sandwich them with eggs and ham. You can also bake them on top of seasonal fruit, as in the berry cobbler on page 178, or present them halved and filled with fruit and whipped cream, for shortcakes. MAKES 10

1½ cups all-purpose flour

¾ cup fine yellow cornmeal

2 tablespoons natural cane sugar

2 teaspoons baking powder

½ teaspoon baking soda

1 teaspoon coarse salt

1 stick (½ cup) unsalted butter, cold, cut into small pieces

1 cup milk

Jam, for serving (optional)

Preheat oven to 375°F. In a large bowl, whisk together flour, cornmeal, sugar, baking powder, baking soda, and salt. Using a pastry blender, cut in butter until mixture resembles coarse meal with a few pea-size pieces remaining.

Pour in milk and mix in with a fork until dough just comes together. The dough will be slightly sticky (do not overmix).

Using two large spoons, drop mounds of dough (about ⅓ cup each) 1½ inches apart on a parchment-lined baking sheet.

Bake, rotating sheet halfway through, until biscuits are golden, 15 to 20 minutes. Slide parchment and biscuits onto a wire rack to cool. Serve warm or at room temperature with jam, if desired. (Biscuits are best the day they're made but can be wrapped and kept at room temperature up to 1 day.)

5 Quick Spreads for Breakfast Breads

A slather of sweet jam or a dollop of creamy yogurt makes muffins, biscuits, and the like that much more tasty and sustaining. Whether you prefer your breakfast sweet or savory, here are five quick, easy-to-prepare spreads to pull together for the morning rush.

1 Stone Fruit Chia Seed Jam

Makes about 2 cups

In a saucepan, combine 1 pound pitted and chopped plums, peaches, nectarines, or apricots with ¼ cup pure maple syrup; cook over medium heat, stirring, until fruit breaks down. Taste and add more syrup, if desired. Stir in 1 tablespoon chia seeds and remove from heat; let stand until thickened, about 10 minutes. Let cool completely. (Jam can be refrigerated up to 2 weeks.)

2 Apple Butter

Makes about 4 cups

Preheat oven to 325°F. In a 9-by-13-inch baking dish, stir together 6½ cups unsweetened applesauce (store-bought or homemade; see recipe page 286), 1¼ cups packed light brown sugar, 1 teaspoon ground cinnamon, and ¼ teaspoon ground allspice. Roast, stirring every 20 minutes, until dark golden brown and reduced to 4 cups, about 1 hour, 50 minutes. Let cool completely. (Apple butter can be refrigerated up to 2 weeks.)

3 Lemony Mashed Avocado with Sesame Seeds

Makes about 1 cup

Using a fork, mash 1 ripe avocado in a bowl; season with salt and pepper. Mix in ½ teaspoon fresh lemon juice and sprinkle with 1 teaspoon toasted sesame seeds. Serve immediately.

4 Garlic-Herb Yogurt

Makes about 2 cups

In a bowl, mix 2 cups Greek yogurt, 2 tablespoons snipped fresh chives, 2 tablespoons finely chopped fresh flat-leaf parsley leaves, and ½ teaspoon minced garlic. Season with ¾ teaspoon coarse salt and freshly ground white pepper. Serve chilled. (Spread can be refrigerated up to 2 days.)

5 Strawberry Coconut Sugar Jam

Makes about 1½ cups

In a saucepan, cook 1 pound hulled and chopped strawberries with ½ cup coconut sugar over medium heat, stirring, until bubbling and thickened, 10 to 15 minutes. Let cool completely. (Jam can be covered and refrigerated up to 1 week.)

Seeded Breakfast Rolls

The seeded rolls served at New York City's Breads Bakery inspired these breakfast buns. Because there are so many add-ins (hazelnuts! dried cherries! and yes, four types of seeds!), each bite is just a little bit different. MAKES 1 DOZEN

For the rolls

- 1 cup warm water (about 110°F)
- 1 envelope (¼ ounce) active dry yeast (2¼ teaspoons)
- 3 tablespoons honey
- 1 large egg, room temperature
- 1¾ cups whole-wheat flour
- 1¾ cups all-purpose flour
- 2 teaspoons coarse salt
- 4 tablespoons unsalted butter, room temperature
- 1 cup hazelnuts, toasted, skinned, and coarsely chopped (see page 288)
- 1 cup dried cherries, chopped
- ¼ cup hulled pumpkin seeds (pepitas)
- ¼ cup sunflower seeds
- 1 tablespoon poppy seeds
- 1 tablespoon black sesame seeds

For the topping

- 1 large egg, lightly beaten
- 2 tablespoons hulled pumpkin seeds (pepitas)
- 2 tablespoons sunflower seeds
- 1 tablespoon poppy seeds
- 1 tablespoon black sesame seeds

Make the rolls: In the bowl of a stand mixer fitted with a dough hook, stir together water, yeast, honey, and egg, and let stand until foamy, 5 minutes. In another bowl, whisk together both flours and salt.

Add the flour mixture to the water mixture, and knead on low until dough is smooth and elastic, 5 minutes. Add butter, 1 tablespoon at a time, and knead until fully incorporated, 4 minutes. Add the nuts, cherries, and seeds, and knead until evenly distributed, 2 minutes.

Turn the dough out onto a work surface, shape into a ball, then return to mixer bowl. Cover with plastic and let rest in a warm spot for 30 minutes. Transfer dough to refrigerator, and let rise at least 8 hours and up to 18 hours.

Turn dough out onto work surface and divide into 12 pieces, about 3¼ ounces each. Gently press each piece into a loosely formed disk, about 3 inches across and 1 inch thick. Arrange evenly spaced on two parchment-lined baking sheets. Loosely cover sheets with plastic and let the dough rise in warm spot until doubled in bulk, about 1 hour.

For the topping: Preheat oven to 375°F. Brush tops and sides of rolls evenly with beaten egg, and sprinkle with seeds. Bake, rotating sheets halfway through, until deep golden, about 22 minutes. Transfer to wire racks and let cool completely before serving.

Whole-Wheat Sticky Buns

The much-loved breakfast treat is now better than ever. With a higher ratio of whole-wheat flour, these brown sugar–glazed sticky buns have a richer, more caramel-like flavor. (The wheat germ adds bit of extra fiber, to boot!) MAKES 10

For the dough

- 2 tablespoons unsalted butter, melted and cooled, plus more for bowl
- 1¼ cups whole-wheat flour
- ¾ cup all-purpose flour, plus more for dusting
- 2 tablespoons toasted wheat germ
- 1⅛ teaspoons active dry yeast (half a ¼-ounce envelope)
- ½ teaspoon coarse salt
- 2 tablespoons packed light brown sugar
- ½ cup warm water (about 110°F)
- 1 large egg

For the filling and topping

- 1 stick (½ cup) unsalted butter, room temperature, plus more for pan
- ¾ cup packed light brown sugar
- ½ teaspoon ground cinnamon
- ½ teaspoon coarse salt
- ½ cup pecans, toasted and chopped (see page 288)

Make the dough: Lightly butter a large bowl. In the bowl of a stand mixer fitted with a dough hook, combine both flours, wheat germ, yeast, salt, brown sugar, water, egg, and melted butter. Knead on medium-low until dough is smooth and elastic, 5 minutes. Transfer to buttered bowl and cover tightly with plastic wrap (see next page for how-to). Let rise in a warm place until doubled in size, about 1 hour.

Make the filling and topping: Butter a 9-inch round cake pan or skillet. In a bowl, stir together butter, brown sugar, cinnamon, and salt until smooth; spread half of mixture over bottom of pan and sprinkle with half of pecans.

Transfer dough to a lightly floured work surface. Gently roll into a 10-by-14-inch rectangle. With an offset spatula, spread remaining sugar mixture on top, leaving a ¼-inch border. Sprinkle with remaining pecans. Starting at a long edge, roll up dough like a jelly roll, then cut crosswise into 10 slices. Place slices in pan cut-side down, spacing evenly. Cover tightly with plastic wrap and let rise in a warm place until buns are just touching, 1 hour.

Preheat oven to 350°F. Bake until buns are golden brown and topping is bubbling around sides of pan, about 25 minutes. Let cool in pan on a wire rack, 15 minutes. With a plate centered over pan, carefully invert buns onto plate. Lift off pan and scrape any remaining topping onto buns. Serve warm. (Assembled, unbaked rolls can be refrigerated overnight. Let stand at room temperature 90 minutes before baking.)

How to Form Sticky Buns

1 Place dough in a lightly buttered bowl, then cover with plastic wrap and let rise in a warm place until doubled in size. **2** With an offset spatula, spread half of filling in buttered pan, then scatter half of chopped pecans over top. **3** On a lightly floured surface, roll dough into a 10-by-14-inch rectangle. **4** With an offset spatula, spread remaining filling over rolled dough, leaving a ¼-inch border.

A buttery sugar-pecan combination doubles as filling and glaze for this easy-to-roll dough.

<u>5</u> With long sides facing you, gently roll up the dough into a tight coil like a jelly roll. <u>6</u> Cut roll crosswise into 10 even slices. <u>7</u> Place slices in prepared pan, cut-side down and spacing evenly. <u>8</u> Cover tightly with plastic wrap and let rise until buns just touch, about 1 hour. Bake as directed.

Oat-and-Millet Granola

Exceptionally crisp and honey-flavored, this seeded granola is a great blue-print for making your own. To spice it up, mix in up to one-half teaspoon ground cinnamon, nutmeg, or cardamom before baking. Or swap in equal amounts of coarsely chopped or whole nuts (almonds, walnuts, hazelnuts, or a combination) for the pumpkin seeds or millet. After the granola has baked and cooled, feel free to add dark chocolate chunks, cocoa nibs, candied ginger, or chopped dried fruit. MAKES 6 CUPS

---

3 cups old-fashioned rolled oats

1 cup large unsweetened coconut flakes

½ cup pumpkin seeds

½ cup millet

2 tablespoons chia seeds

2 tablespoons sesame seeds

¼ cup extra-virgin olive oil or melted virgin coconut oil

¼ cup honey or pure maple syrup

¼ cup packed light brown sugar

½ teaspoon coarse salt

Preheat oven to 300°F. In a large bowl, combine all ingredients and stir until grains and seeds are well coated. Spread evenly on a rimmed baking sheet.

Bake, stirring occasionally and rotating sheet halfway through, until deep golden brown, about 45 minutes. Let cool completely before transferring to an airtight container. (Granola can be stored in an airtight container at room temperature up to 2 weeks.)

Mixed-Seed Clusters

Full of sesame seeds, anise seeds, pumpkin seeds, and flaxseeds, as well as pistachios and honey, these chunky clusters are as perfect sprinkled over your morning yogurt as they are your evening ice cream. You can also keep them at your desk for a midday snack. MAKES ABOUT 6½ CUPS

1¼ cups old-fashioned rolled oats

1 cup chopped shelled unsalted pistachios

½ cup packed light brown sugar

¼ cup sesame seeds

2 tablespoons anise seeds

½ cup hulled pumpkin seeds (pepitas)

½ cup flaxseed meal (ground flaxseeds)

1 teaspoon coarse salt

⅓ cup honey

¼ cup extra-virgin olive oil

2 large egg whites, whisked

Preheat oven to 300°F. In a large bowl, combine all ingredients and toss until grains and seeds are well coated. Spread mixture on a rimmed baking sheet, patting into an even ¼-inch-thick layer.

Bake, rotating sheet halfway through, 35 minutes. Use a wide spatula to flip in large sections. Flatten back into a single layer and bake 10 minutes longer. Let sheet cool completely on a wire rack.

Scrape up baked seed mixture with spatula and break into chunks. (Clusters can be stored in an airtight container at room temperature up to 1 week.)

Breakfast Cookies

Quick-cooking oats form the base of these tender cinnamon-spiced cookies. With buckwheat flour, millet, cashew butter, coconut oil, and fresh raspberries, the treats should keep you well-fueled throughout the morning. Think of them as your breakfast bowl to go. MAKES ABOUT 28

2 cups quick-cooking oats

½ cup buckwheat flour

½ cup millet

¾ teaspoon ground cinnamon

1 teaspoon baking soda

¾ teaspoon coarse salt

1 cup cashew butter

½ cup virgin coconut oil

¾ cup packed light brown sugar

2 large eggs

1 cup fresh raspberries

Yogurt, for serving (optional)

Preheat oven to 375°F. In a large bowl, whisk together oats, buckwheat flour, millet, cinnamon, baking soda, and salt.

In a saucepan, heat cashew butter, coconut oil, and brown sugar, stirring, just until smooth and combined. Pour over oat mixture and stir until incorporated. Let cool to warm.

Stir in eggs, then fold in raspberries (it's okay if they break apart slightly).

Scoop 2-tablespoon mounds of dough onto parchment-lined baking sheets. Using your hands or the bottom of a glass, flatten cookies slightly. Bake, rotating sheets halfway through, until light golden brown and set, 15 to 18 minutes. Transfer sheets to racks and let cookies cool completely. Serve with yogurt, if desired. (Cookies can be kept in an airtight container at room temperature up to 2 days.)

Coconut Baked Oatmeal

As rich as cream but free of dairy, coconut milk (along with an egg) makes this porridge custardy and pudding-like, with delicious crisp-chewy edges. Feel free to swap in different spices in place of the ginger—a mix of cinnamon, cardamom, and nutmeg is nice. SERVES 6

Virgin coconut oil, for pan

2 cups old-fashioned rolled oats

½ cup large unsweetened coconut flakes

⅓ cup plus 1 tablespoon packed light brown sugar

1 teaspoon ground ginger

½ teaspoon coarse salt

1 teaspoon baking powder

1 can (13.5 ounces) unsweetened coconut milk

¼ cup water

1 large egg

2 teaspoons vanilla extract

8 ounces fresh figs, stemmed and quartered, or 4 ounces small, ripe plums, thinly sliced

Pure maple syrup, for serving (optional)

Preheat oven to 375°F with rack in lower third of oven. Oil an 8-inch square baking pan.

In a bowl, combine oats, coconut flakes, ⅓ cup brown sugar, the ginger, salt, and baking powder. In a separate bowl, whisk together coconut milk, the water, egg, and vanilla. Add egg mixture to oat mixture and stir just to combine.

Pour oatmeal into prepared baking pan and top with sliced figs. Sprinkle remaining 1 tablespoon brown sugar over top and bake, rotating pan halfway through, 35 to 40 minutes, until top is nicely golden and oat mixture has set. Let cool slightly. Serve with maple syrup, if desired.

Swiss Chard and Sausage Strata

A strata is like a savory bread pudding and stands as the ultimate make-ahead dish for savory breakfast lovers—you can assemble the ingredients the night before and bake it in the morning. Here, whole-grain bread replaces the usual white bread. Instead of bulk sausage, you can use Italian sausage links and remove the meat from the casing. SERVES 8

1 pound bulk sweet or spicy Italian sausage

1 tablespoon extra-virgin olive oil

2 shallots, finely chopped

1 bunch Swiss chard (1 pound), stems chopped, leaves torn into 2-inch pieces and rinsed

Coarse salt and freshly ground pepper

1 (10-ounce) loaf crust-on whole-grain bread, cut into 10 slices

2½ cups milk

7 large eggs, lightly beaten

3 ounces Gruyère cheese, coarsely grated (1 cup)

Variations

You can swap in cheddar or fontina for the Gruyère; spinach or kale for the Swiss chard; and 4 ounces ham or speck (neither needs pre-cooking) for the 1 pound sausage. For a completely vegetarian filling, sauté 1 pound mushrooms with the shallots to use in place of sausage.

Preheat oven to 375°F. In a large skillet, cook sausage over medium heat, breaking up meat with a spoon, until browned, 5 minutes. Transfer sausage to a small bowl; discard fat. Heat olive oil in skillet over medium and add shallots and chard stems to skillet; cook until shallots are translucent, 3 minutes. Add a little water to pan and cook, stirring and scraping up browned bits from skillet with spoon. Add chard leaves and cook, stirring occasionally, until wilted, 3 minutes. Season with salt and pepper.

Spread half the sausage in a 9-by-13-inch baking dish and top with half the chard mixture. Top with bread, overlapping slices slightly. Top with remaining sausage and chard mixture. In a large bowl, whisk together milk and eggs, season with salt and pepper, and pour evenly over bread. Firmly press to submerge bread in egg mixture. Cover dish tightly with parchment followed by foil and let stand 10 minutes (or refrigerate up to overnight).

Bake, rotating pan halfway through, for 45 minutes. Uncover, sprinkle with cheese, and bake until cheese melts and egg mixture is mostly absorbed and set in center, 5 to 10 minutes. Let cool 10 minutes before serving.

Cookies, Brownies, and Bars

Seeded Graham Biscotti

Coconut-Pistachio Biscotti

Oatmeal Shortbread

Granola Cookies

Pecan, Oat, and Dark Chocolate Chunk Cookies

Farro Chocolate-Chunk Cookies

Flourless Double-Chocolate Pecan Cookies

Chewy Molasses Crinkles

Half-Moon Cookies

Whole-Wheat Snickerdoodle Bites

Almond-Rye Heart Cookies

Spelt-Nut Crescents

Whole-Wheat Almond-Butter Sandwich Cookies

Cashew Butter and Jam Thumbprints

Buckwheat-Espresso Cookies

Almond-Coconut Macaroons

Dark Chocolate–Spelt Brownies

Gluten-Free Fudgy Pecan Brownies

Whole-Wheat Fig Crumble Squares

Spelt Honey-Cashew Blondies

Vegan Lemon-Coconut Squares

Cherry-Date Oat Bars

Sweet Oat-Walnut Crisps

Fruit and Honey Nut Bars

Graham Crackers

Amaranth Clusters

Seeded Graham Biscotti

Hemp seeds, aromatic fennel seeds, and a double dose of vanilla (seeds and extract) flavor these almond-studded twice-baked cookies. Before they're baked for the first time, they're rolled in a mixture of raw sugar and sesame seeds for more crunch. The biscotti are lovely made with regular whole-wheat flour, but it's worth seeking out graham flour. Try a few with an afternoon espresso.
MAKES 3 DOZEN

1⅓ cups all-purpose flour

¾ cup graham flour or whole-wheat flour

1 teaspoon baking powder

1 teaspoon baking soda

¾ teaspoon coarse salt

¼ teaspoon ground allspice

¼ cup hemp seeds

1 tablespoon fennel seeds

¾ cup packed light brown sugar

2 large eggs, room temperature

1 vanilla bean, split lengthwise, seeds scraped

1 teaspoon vanilla extract

1 teaspoon finely grated orange zest

¾ cup whole almonds, toasted (see page 288)

2 tablespoons raw sugar, such as turbinado

2 tablespoons sesame seeds

Preheat oven to 350°F. In a bowl, whisk together both flours, baking powder, baking soda, salt, allspice, and hemp and fennel seeds. In another bowl, with an electric mixer, beat brown sugar, eggs, vanilla seeds and extract, and zest on medium until pale and thickened, about 4 minutes. With mixer on low, add flour mixture and beat until combined. Fold in almonds.

Shape dough into a 12-by-3-inch log. Combine turbinado sugar and sesame seeds on a rimmed baking sheet; roll log in mixture to completely coat. Transfer to a parchment-lined baking sheet; bake, rotating sheet halfway through, until golden, about 30 minutes. Transfer sheet to a wire rack and let log cool completely.

Transfer log to a cutting board. Using a serrated knife, cut crosswise into ⅓-inch-thick slices. Transfer slices to baking sheet and bake, rotating sheet halfway through, until golden brown, about 10 minutes. Let cool completely on sheet on wire rack before serving. (Biscotti can be kept in an airtight container at room temperature up to 1 week.)

Coconut-Pistachio Biscotti

Here's a novel and tasty biscotti. At first glance they seem to be pretty classically Italian, with the combination of cornmeal, olive oil, lemon, and pistachio. But coconut and sweet-tart dried cherries add even more flavor and interest. Wrap the biscotti in cellophane bags for sweet, wholesome gifts—but be sure to keep some around for whenever you need a treat. MAKES 2 DOZEN

1 cup all-purpose flour

1 cup medium-grind cornmeal

½ cup unsweetened shredded coconut

½ teaspoon baking powder

½ teaspoon coarse salt

2 large eggs

¾ cup natural cane sugar

¼ cup plus 2 tablespoons extra-virgin olive oil

1 tablespoon finely grated lemon zest

1 cup unsweetened dried cherries

1 cup shelled unsalted pistachios

Preheat oven to 350°F. In a large bowl, whisk together flour, cornmeal, coconut, baking powder, and salt. In another bowl, with an electric mixer, beat eggs, sugar, oil, and zest on medium until well combined. With mixer on low, add flour mixture, and beat until just combined. Fold in cherries and pistachios.

Transfer dough to a parchment-lined baking sheet, and shape into a 14-by-4-inch log. Bake, rotating sheet halfway through, until firm and golden, 30 to 35 minutes. Transfer to a wire rack, and let log cool completely. Reduce oven temperature to 325°F.

Transfer log to a cutting board. Using a serrated knife, cut diagonally into ½-inch-thick slices. Transfer slices to baking sheets and bake, rotating sheets halfway through, until just golden around the edges, 15 to 18 minutes. Let cool completely on sheets on wire racks. (Biscotti can be kept in an airtight container at room temperature up to 1 week.)

Oatmeal Shortbread

One of the virtues of shortbread is that it's made with so few ingredients: This recipe pulls its inspiration from shortbread's home country—Scotland—where oats are a staple. Both ground into a flour and used as a topping, toasted oats help create a sweet, mellow flavor and perfect crumbly texture. Bake these and sprinkle with oatmeal, as directed, or add something more flavorful on top, like crystallized ginger (far left) or pink peppercorns (center). MAKES 32

½ cup plus 2 tablespoons old-fashioned rolled oats

¾ cup all-purpose flour

⅓ cup confectioners' sugar

½ teaspoon coarse salt

1 stick (½ cup) cold unsalted butter, cut into pieces

Crushed pink peppercorns or diced crystallized ginger, for sprinkling (optional)

Preheat oven to 325°F. Spread oats on a rimmed baking sheet. Toast until fragrant and lightly browned, 4 to 6 minutes. Let cool completely.

In a food processor, process flour, sugar, salt, and ½ cup cooled oats until finely ground. Add butter and pulse just until mixture is the consistency of coarse meal. Transfer to an 8-inch square baking pan; press firmly into bottom. Sprinkle remaining oats on top and press gently. Sprinkle with pink peppercorns or crystallized ginger, if desired.

Bake, rotating pan halfway through, until shortbread is firm and lightly browned, 30 to 35 minutes. Using a paring knife, immediately score shortbread into 16 squares; then score each square diagonally into 2 triangles. Transfer pan to a wire rack and let shortbread cool completely. Gently remove shortbread, and break along scored lines. (Shortbread can be kept in an airtight container at room temperature up to 5 days.)

Granola Cookies

Coconut oil takes the place of butter in this brown-sugar-based dough. Wholesome granola mix-ins—coconut flakes, dried cherries, pepitas—are added alongside bittersweet chocolate chunks for an irresistible old-fashioned drop cookie that's a great energy-boosting snack. MAKES ABOUT 40

- ½ cup virgin coconut oil
- 1 cup packed light brown sugar
- 2 large eggs
- 1 teaspoon vanilla extract
- 1¼ cups all-purpose flour
- ½ teaspoon baking soda
- 1 teaspoon coarse salt
- ½ cup old-fashioned rolled oats
- ¼ cup flaxseed meal (ground flaxseeds)
- ½ cup hulled pumpkin seeds (pepitas)
- ¾ cup large unsweetened coconut flakes
- 5 ounces bittersweet chocolate, coarsely chopped (about 1 cup)
- 1 cup unsweetened dried cherries or cranberries, chopped

In a bowl, with an electric mixer, beat oil and brown sugar on medium until well combined, about 3 minutes. Beat in eggs and vanilla. Add flour, baking soda, and salt, and beat until combined. Stir in oats, flaxseed meal, pumpkin seeds, coconut, chocolate, and cherries until well combined. Refrigerate dough until firm, about 1 hour.

Preheat oven to 350°F. Drop heaping tablespoons of dough, 2 inches apart, onto parchment-lined baking sheets. Bake, rotating sheets halfway through, until golden, 13 to 14 minutes. Transfer sheets to wire racks and let cookies cool completely. (Cookies can be kept in airtight containers at room temperature up to 2 days.)

To make the cookie whole grain, swap in spelt flour for the all-purpose. To make gluten-free, substitute 1 cup of Wholesome Flour from Cup 4 Cup (available at cup4cup.com) for the all-purpose, and use gluten-free oats.

Pecan, Oat, and Dark Chocolate Chunk Cookies

It's hard to believe that a vegan cookie could taste so extraordinary. These chunky cookies are chock-full of oats and bits of dark chocolate and are as satisfying as any giant, buttery bakery-style chocolate chip cookie. The pecans here are ground fine, so they act as the flour, while maple syrup is the primary sweetener. MAKES 10

---

2 cups pecans, chopped

1 cup old-fashioned rolled oats

¾ teaspoon baking powder

½ teaspoon coarse salt

½ teaspoon cornstarch

¼ cup extra-virgin olive oil

¼ cup maple syrup

½ teaspoon pure vanilla extract

3 ounces dark chocolate, chopped into ¼ inch pieces (½ cup)

Preheat oven to 325°F. Working in 2 batches, process pecans in a food processor until just finely ground (do not overprocess to a paste). Transfer to a bowl, and stir in oats, baking powder, salt, and cornstarch. Make a well in the center, and add olive oil, maple syrup, and vanilla. Stir to combine (dough will be sticky and a bit crumbly). Fold in chocolate.

Line a baking sheet with parchment. Scoop and firmly pack dough using a ¼ measuring cup. Transfer dough to baking sheet, then flatten slightly with damp hands until ½ inch thick. Repeat with remaining dough.

Bake, rotating sheet halfway through, until light golden, about 20 minutes. Transfer baking sheet to a wire rack and let cookies cool completely. (Cookies will crisp as they cool.)

Farro Chocolate-Chunk Cookies

The whole-wheat chocolate chip cookie from the book *Good to the Grain*, by pastry chef Kim Boyce, inspired this recipe, which relies on farro flour. (You can use spelt or regular whole-wheat, if you prefer.) With fruit, nuts, and chocolate chunks in every bite, these cookies are perfect for the countertop jar. MAKES ABOUT 40

- 3 cups farro flour
- 1¼ teaspoons baking powder
- ¼ teaspoon baking soda
- 1 teaspoon coarse salt
- 2 sticks (1 cup) unsalted butter, room temperature
- 2 cups packed dark brown sugar
- 2 teaspoons vanilla extract
- 2 large eggs
- 1½ cups coarsely chopped semisweet chocolate
- 1 cup coarsely chopped walnuts
- 1 cup coarsely chopped dried fruit, such as dates or raisins (optional)

Preheat oven to 325°F. In a bowl, whisk together flour, baking powder, baking soda, and salt. In a large bowl, with an electric mixer, beat butter with brown sugar on medium-high until fluffy, about 2 minutes. Add vanilla, then eggs, one at a time, beating to combine after each. With a mixer on low, gradually beat in flour mixture until just combined. Add chocolate, walnuts, and fruit, if desired, and beat to combine.

Scoop 2-tablespoon mounds of dough about 2 inches apart on parchment-lined baking sheets. Bake, rotating sheets halfway through, until cookies are just set on top, about 15 minutes. Transfer sheets to wire racks and let cookies cool completely. (Cookies can be kept in airtight containers at room temperature up to 3 days.)

5 Tips for Baking with Chocolate

Just as the variety of flours and sweeteners has greatly expanded, there are now more types of and classifications for chocolate than ever. Here are a few things to keep in mind as you consider your options.

1 Chop your own.

For most recipes, we prefer to chop quality chocolate bars ourselves rather than use chips. Most chips contain a lot of an emulsifier to help them keep their shape as they bake; this can make the chocolate less flavorful. We also prefer the more rustic look of hand-chopped chunks.

2 Know the percentages.

These days, many chocolate labels include the percentage of cocoa matter (often called cacao) in a bar. The cocoa matter includes the flavorful cocoa powder, as well as the fatty, nearly flavorless cocoa butter. In this book, the recipes call for semisweet, bittersweet, and dark chocolate—words that are often used interchangeably. For semisweet, that means 45 to 55 percent cacao; for bittersweet, between 56 and 70 percent cacao; and dark, more than 70 percent. Feel free to use the type of chocolate you like best.

3 Choose wisely.

Chocolate brands often tout words and phrases such as *organic* and *fair trade* on their packaging; some even include where the cocoa beans originated. *Organic chocolate* means the cocoa beans were grown without the use of synthetic pesticides and conventional fertilizers and that it also contains other organic ingredients. *Fair trade* means farmers received a fair wage for their crop. Many companies work in environmentally and socially responsible ways without having official certification; it's best to research the company behind the chocolate if you'd like to learn more.

4 Use the right cocoa powders.

Natural cocoa retains chocolate's acidity and slight reddish tinge while Dutch process is treated with an alkalizing agent to make it darker and richer tasting (this is our preference for most baked goods). Keep in mind that Dutch-process cocoa powder isn't acidic, so it won't react with baking soda; be careful when making a swap in recipes that contain baking soda.

5 Consider the cocoa nib.

Think of nibs—unsweetened bits of fermented cocoa beans—as the new chocolate chips. Even though they're not sweet, they pack an intense chocolate flavor and delightful crunch that's just right in cookies, granolas, and brownies. You can find them at specialty food shops, in some grocery stores, and online.

Flourless Double-Chocolate Pecan Cookies

Confectioners' sugar, cocoa powder, and egg whites provide the structure for these gluten-free cookies, which have the chewiness of a meringue with the chocolaty flavor of a brownie. We love the rich flavor of Dutch-process cocoa powder here, but natural cocoa powder works equally well. MAKES 1 DOZEN

- 3 cups confectioners' sugar
- ¾ cup unsweetened cocoa powder
- ½ teaspoon coarse salt
- 5 ounces bittersweet chocolate, chopped
- 1½ cups chopped pecans
- 4 large egg whites, room temperature

Preheat oven to 325°F. In a large bowl, whisk together sugar, cocoa powder, and salt. Stir in chocolate and pecans. Add egg whites and stir just until incorporated (do not overmix).

Line a baking sheet with parchment. Scoop and firmly pack dough using a ¼ measuring cup. Transfer dough to baking sheet, spacing cookies about 3 inches apart.

Bake, rotating sheets halfway through, until cookie tops are dry and crackled, about 25 minutes. Transfer sheets to wire racks and let cookies cool completely. (Cookies can be kept in an airtight container at room temperature up to 3 days.)

Chewy Molasses Crinkles

Nearly as beloved as the chocolate chip cookie, gingery molasses cookies are a must-have in every baker's repertoire. This chewy-crisp version of the cookie jar favorite gets an update with quinoa flour, which lends a pleasing background note that's delicious with the assertive molasses and spices.

MAKES ABOUT 2 DOZEN

1 stick (½ cup) unsalted butter, room temperature

1 cup packed light brown sugar

½ cup natural cane sugar

2 large eggs

½ cup unsulfured molasses

2 tablespoons safflower oil

1½ cups all-purpose flour

½ cup quinoa flour

1 teaspoon baking soda

1 teaspoon ground cinnamon

1 teaspoon ground ginger

1 teaspoon ground allspice

½ teaspoon coarse salt

½ cup raw sugar, such as turbinado, for rolling

In a bowl, with an electric mixer, beat butter, brown sugar, and cane sugar on medium until smooth, about 3 minutes. Mix in eggs, one at a time, followed by the molasses and oil.

With mixer on low, gradually mix in flours, baking soda, cinnamon, ginger, allspice, and salt. Cover dough with plastic wrap and refrigerate until firm, about 1 hour or up to overnight.

Preheat oven to 325°F. Put raw sugar in a bowl. Roll 2 tablespoons of dough into a ball; repeat for remaining dough. Roll balls in sugar to coat, and space 3 inches apart on parchment-lined baking sheets.

Bake, rotating sheets halfway through, until cookies are flat and centers are set, 14 to 16 minutes. Transfer sheets to wire rack and let cookies cool completely. (Cookies can be stored between layers of parchment in an airtight container at room temperature up to 5 days.)

Half-Moon Cookies

These black-and-white cookies are about a quarter the size of the bakery versions and are made with a substantial amount of whole-wheat flour. Plus some of the basic white glaze is tinted with berries instead of food coloring for charming pink-and-white versions. MAKES ABOUT 20 MEDIUM OR 34 MINI

¾ cup all-purpose flour

½ cup whole-wheat flour

½ teaspoon baking soda

¾ teaspoon coarse salt

6 tablespoons unsalted butter, room temperature

½ cup plus 1 tablespoon natural cane sugar

1 large egg

½ teaspoon vanilla extract

⅓ cup buttermilk

¾ cup fresh raspberries

2 cups confectioners' sugar

1 tablespoon plus 1 teaspoon honey

1 teaspoon fresh lemon juice

Water, for the glaze

1½ teaspoons unsweetened cocoa powder

In a bowl, whisk together both flours, baking soda, and salt. In another bowl, with an electric mixer, beat butter on medium until smooth, about 2 minutes. Add ½ cup cane sugar, and beat until pale and fluffy, about 3 minutes. Beat in egg and vanilla. With mixer on low, add flour mixture in three batches, alternating with two additions of buttermilk, beating until just combined (do not overmix). Refrigerate until firm, about 1 hour.

Preheat oven to 350°F. Roll 1 or 1½ tablespoon pieces of dough into balls; place 2 inches apart on parchment-lined baking sheets. Bake, rotating sheets halfway through, until bottoms turn golden, about 10 minutes. Transfer cookies to wire racks and let cool completely.

In a saucepan, cook berries and remaining 1 tablespoon granulated sugar over medium-high heat, stirring until juices have been released. Pass mixture through a fine sieve into a bowl and let cool.

Whisk together confectioners' sugar, honey, lemon juice, and 2 tablespoons water in a small bowl. Transfer half the icing to another bowl, and whisk in 1 teaspoon more water. Divide remaining portion in half again, and stir ½ teaspoon berry puree into one part, and cocoa powder and ¾ teaspoon water into the other. Spread white icing on half of each cookie's flat side and berry or chocolate icing on other half. Let set 30 minutes before serving.

Whole-Wheat Snickerdoodle Bites

The beloved cinnamon-dusted snickerdoodle goes bite-size, each made with just one teaspoon of dough. The recipe includes both whole-wheat flour and wheat germ, and yields an impressive 12 dozen little cookies. They are perfect packed three or four to a bag for a bake sale. MAKES ABOUT 12 DOZEN

1¼ cups all-purpose flour

1 cup whole-wheat flour

¼ cup toasted wheat germ

2 teaspoons cream of tartar

1 teaspoon baking soda

½ teaspoon coarse salt

2 sticks (1 cup) unsalted butter, room temperature

1¾ cups natural cane sugar

2 large eggs

1 tablespoon ground cinnamon

In a bowl, whisk together both flours, wheat germ, cream of tartar, baking soda, and salt. In another bowl, with an electric mixer, beat butter with 1½ cups sugar on medium-high until pale and fluffy, about 3 minutes. Add eggs, one at a time, beating to combine after each. Gradually beat in flour mixture until combined. Refrigerate dough until firm, about 30 minutes.

Preheat oven to 350°F. Combine remaining ¼ cup sugar and the cinnamon in a small bowl. Roll teaspoons of dough into balls, then roll in cinnamon sugar to coat. Transfer to parchment-lined baking sheets, spacing 1½ inches apart.

Bake, rotating sheets halfway through, until golden, about 10 minutes. Transfer cookies to a wire rack and let cool completely. (Cookies can be kept in an airtight container at room temperature up to 3 days.)

Almond-Rye Heart Cookies

Rye flour and ground toasted almonds lend a delicate sweetness to these cookies, with a dash of almond extract thrown in for more flavor. Using confectioners' sugar in the dough makes them extra crisp. Rolling the dough into ropes and forming them into hearts is easier (and less wasteful) than rolling and cutting out dough with cutters. Dusted with confectioners' sugar, they're a sweet treat for Valentine's Day—or any day. MAKES ABOUT 2 DOZEN

½ cup blanched whole almonds, toasted (see page 288)

½ cup light rye flour

½ cup all-purpose flour

¼ teaspoon coarse salt

¼ teaspoon ground cinnamon

1 stick (½ cup) unsalted butter, room temperature

½ cup confectioners' sugar, plus more for dusting

1 large egg yolk

¼ teaspoon almond extract

In a food processor, pulse almonds and both flours until nuts are finely ground. Add salt and cinnamon; pulse to combine.

In a bowl, with an electric mixer, beat together butter and sugar on medium until smooth and fluffy, about 2 minutes. Add egg yolk and almond extract, and beat until combined. With mixer on low, gradually beat in flour mixture until just combined.

Preheat oven to 350°F. Roll tablespoon-size portions of dough into ¼-inch-thick ropes, each about 7 inches long. Transfer to parchment-lined baking sheets, and shape into hearts. Refrigerate until firm, about 10 minutes.

Bake, rotating sheets halfway through, until cookies are golden brown and crisp, about 17 minutes. Transfer sheets to wire racks and let cookies cool completely. Dust with confectioners' sugar just before serving. (Cookies can be kept in an airtight container at room temperature up to 3 days.)

Spelt-Nut Crescents

Spelt's sweet-spice flavor is perfect in these nutty Viennese-style holiday classics. If you can't find blanched hazelnuts, toast the nuts and then remove the skins yourself. If you prefer, you can substitute walnuts or more almonds for the hazelnuts. MAKES ABOUT 30

1½ cups spelt flour

½ cup blanched whole hazelnuts, toasted (see page 288)

¾ cup blanched whole almonds, toasted (see page 288)

¼ teaspoon salt

1½ sticks (¾ cup) unsalted butter, room temperature

1½ cups confectioners' sugar

1 teaspoon vanilla extract

In a food processor, combine ½ cup flour with nuts and pulse until nuts are finely ground. In a bowl, whisk together flour-nut mixture and remaining 1 cup flour and the salt.

In a bowl, with an electric mixer, beat butter and ½ cup sugar on medium-high until pale and fluffy, about 2 minutes. Beat in vanilla. With mixer on low, add flour mixture in two batches, and beat until combined.

Roll a tablespoon-size portion of dough into a 3-inch log. Using your fingers, shape log into a crescent, tapering the ends slightly so the center is the widest part. Repeat with remaining dough, spacing crescents about 1 inch apart on parchment-lined baking sheets. Freeze or refrigerate until crescents are very firm, about 30 minutes.

Preheat oven to 350°F. Bake, rotating sheets halfway through, until edges of cookies begin to turn golden, 16 to 18 minutes. Transfer sheets to wire racks to cool 5 minutes, then transfer cookies to racks to cool completely. Roll cookies in remaining 1 cup sugar. (Cookies can be kept in an airtight container at room temperature up to 5 days.)

Whole-Wheat Almond-Butter Sandwich Cookies

Made with almond butter and toasted almonds, these cookies, which rely completely on whole-wheat pastry flour, are a scrumptious riff on the beloved peanut-butter sandwich cookie. The delightfully crisp almond cookies are also tasty all on their own. MAKES 30 SANDWICHES

1¼ cups whole-wheat pastry flour

1 teaspoon baking soda

¾ teaspoon coarse salt

1 stick (½ cup) unsalted butter, room temperature

½ cup smooth natural unsalted almond butter, well stirred

1 cup packed light brown sugar

1 large egg

1 cup sliced almonds, toasted and finely chopped (see page 288)

16 ounces cream cheese, room temperature

¼ cup honey

½ teaspoon vanilla extract

In a bowl, whisk together flour, baking soda, and salt. In another bowl, with an electric mixer, beat butter on medium-high, 1 minute. Add almond butter, and beat until smooth. Beat in brown sugar, then egg, until well mixed. With mixer on low, gradually add flour mixture until just combined. Stir in almonds.

Form dough into a log roughly 11 inches long and 1¾ inches in diameter. Wrap in parchment, and freeze until firm, about 1 hour (or up to 3 months).

Preheat oven to 350°F. Using a chef's knife, slice log into scant ¼-inch-thick rounds, using one quick motion for each slice. (For easier slicing, keep log frozen between batches of cookies.) Arrange rounds 1½ inches apart on parchment-lined baking sheets, pressing back into shape as needed.

Bake, rotating sheets halfway through, until cookies are light golden on edges, 8 to 10 minutes. Transfer sheets to wire racks and let cookies cool completely.

With an electric mixer, beat cream cheese, honey, and vanilla on medium until combined. Spread 1 tablespoon each on the bottoms of half the cookies, then sandwich with remaining cookies, pressing gently to spread filling. (Filled cookies are best the same day.)

Cashew Butter and Jam Thumbprints

Cashew butter gets blended with sugar, egg, and salt to make a flourless, dairy-free cookie dough. Pressed into mini cookies and filled with jam, these are an adorably sweet take on PB&J. You can use any combination of nut butter and jam: We like cashew butter with raspberry; almond butter with apricot; and peanut butter with strawberry. MAKES ABOUT 3 DOZEN

1 cup unsweetened cashew butter

1 cup natural cane sugar

1 large egg

½ teaspoon baking soda

¼ teaspoon coarse salt

¼ cup jam or jelly

Preheat oven to 350°F. In a large bowl, stir together cashew butter, sugar, egg, baking soda, and salt. Scoop 2 teaspoons of dough and roll into ball; repeat with remaining dough.

Transfer to parchment-lined baking sheets and flatten balls into disks about ¼ inch thick.

Bake cookies until golden and set around edges, about 7 minutes. Remove from oven and use a ¼ teaspoon measure to create a well in the center of each cookie.

Return sheets to oven and bake, rotating sheets halfway through, about 7 minutes longer, until cookies are lightly golden. Transfer sheets to wire racks and let cookies cool completely. Fill with ¼ teaspoon jam or jelly. (Cookies can be kept in an airtight container at room temperature up to 1 week.)

Buckwheat-Espresso Cookies

Buckwheat flour can often overpower other flavors, but that's not the case here. Inspired by a recipe from Matt Dillon of Seattle's Sitka and Spruce restaurant, these crisp, sandy, slice-and-bake cookies taste intriguingly grown-up; the buckwheat flour brings out the pleasantly bitter flavors in coffee and cocoa nibs. Keep them on hand for an afternoon pick-me-up. MAKES 30

1½ cups all-purpose flour

¾ cup buckwheat flour

¼ teaspoon coarse salt

1 tablespoon instant espresso powder

2 sticks (1 cup) unsalted butter, room temperature

⅔ cup natural cane sugar

⅓ cup cocoa nibs, plus more for sprinkling

1½ teaspoons vanilla extract

In a bowl, whisk together both flours, salt, and espresso powder. In a large bowl, with an electric mixer, beat together butter and sugar on medium-high until pale and fluffy, about 4 minutes. With mixer on low, gradually add flour mixture, beating until just combined. Add cocoa nibs and vanilla, and beat until just combined.

Transfer dough to a work surface and gently knead a few times to evenly distribute nibs. Form dough into a log roughly 12 inches long and 1½ inches in diameter. Tightly wrap log in parchment, and refrigerate until firm, at least 1 hour and up to 1 day.

Preheat oven to 325°F and set racks in upper and lower thirds of the oven. Unwrap dough and slice into rounds ¼ inch thick. Arrange rounds 1 inch apart on parchment-lined baking sheets.

Bake, rotating sheets halfway through, until lightly golden, 13 to 15 minutes. Transfer cookies to a wire rack and let cool completely. Cookies will become firm and crisp as they cool. (Cookies can be kept in an airtight container at room temperature up to 3 days.)

Almond-Coconut Macaroons

You won't find an easier treat to prepare from scratch. These are made with only a handful of pantry items, including unsweetened coconut and almonds, both good sources of healthy fats. The result: a gluten-free treat that's crisp and nutty with a chewy center. If you'd like to add chocolate, replace the almonds with chocolate chunks or dip the baked macaroons in melted chocolate. The pyramid shape of these cookies creates delightfully browned, crisp edges, but you can simply form into mounds if you prefer. MAKES 2 DOZEN

1 cup natural cane sugar

3 large egg whites

3 cups unsweetened shredded coconut

¾ cup slivered almonds

1½ teaspoons vanilla extract

½ teaspoon coarse salt

Preheat oven to 350°F. In a bowl, whisk together sugar and egg whites. Stir in the coconut, almonds, vanilla, and salt.

Scoop 2-tablespoon mounds of almond mixture onto parchment-lined baking sheets, spacing about 2 inches apart. With moistened hands, squeeze mounds tightly together two or three times to form a compact ball. Using a spatula, flatten one side at a time to form a pyramid shape.

Bake, rotating sheets halfway through, until golden brown on bottoms and edges, about 15 minutes. Transfer sheets to wire racks and let cool 5 minutes, then transfer macaroons to racks and let cool completely. (Macaroons can be stored in an airtight container at room temperature up to 1 week.)

Dark Chocolate–Spelt Brownies

These double-chocolate, chewy one-bowl brownies develop depth with hints of maple, thanks to the spelt flour. The secret to a shiny, crackly crust? After adding the eggs, beat the batter for one minute. MAKES 16

- 1 stick (½ cup) unsalted cold butter, cut into tablespoons, plus more for pan
- 6 ounces dark chocolate, preferably 70 percent cacao, chopped (about 1¼ cups)
- ¾ cup natural cane sugar
- ¾ cup packed light brown sugar
- 3 large eggs, room temperature
- ¼ cup unsweetened cocoa powder
- ½ teaspoon coarse salt
- ¾ cup spelt flour

Preheat oven to 350°F. Lightly butter an 8-inch square baking pan. Line with parchment, leaving a 2-inch overhang on two sides. Butter parchment.

Place butter and chocolate in a large heatproof bowl set over a saucepan of simmering water, and melt, stirring, until smooth. Remove from heat, and whisk in both sugars. Whisk in eggs, one at a time, until combined. Beat batter vigorously for 1 minute. Whisk in cocoa and salt; then fold in flour until combined.

Pour batter into pan and smooth top. Bake, rotating pan halfway through, until a tester inserted in center comes out with a few moist crumbs, about 35 minutes. Let cool completely in pan on a wire rack. Using paper overhang, lift cake out of pan and transfer to a cutting board; cut into 16 squares. (Brownies can be stored in an airtight container at room temperature up to 3 days.)

Gluten-Free Fudgy Pecan Brownies

Cornstarch helps lighten the texture of these brownies the way flour would while still keeping them fudgy. If you want to boost the chocolate flavor even more, mix one-quarter cup cocoa nibs into the batter and sprinkle more on top. MAKES 16

- 6 tablespoons unsalted butter, cut into pieces, plus more for pan
- ⅓ cup cornstarch
- ¼ cup unsweetened Dutch-process cocoa powder
- ¼ teaspoon ground cinnamon
- ½ teaspoon fine salt
- 12 ounces semisweet chocolate, finely chopped
- ¾ cup natural cane sugar
- 1 teaspoon vanilla extract
- 3 large eggs
- 1 cup chopped toasted pecans (see page 288)

Preheat oven to 350°F. Lightly butter an 8-inch square baking pan and line with parchment, leaving a 2-inch overhang on two sides. Butter parchment.

In a bowl, whisk together cornstarch, cocoa, cinnamon, and salt. Place butter and chocolate in a large heatproof bowl set over a saucepan of simmering water, and melt, stirring, until smooth. Remove from heat and whisk in sugar and vanilla. Whisk in eggs, one at a time, until combined. Add cornstarch mixture, and stir vigorously until mixture is smooth and begins to pull away from side of bowl, about 2 minutes. Fold in pecans.

Pour batter into pan and smooth top. Bake, rotating pan halfway through, until a tester inserted in center comes out with a few moist crumbs, about 35 minutes. Let cool completely in pan on a wire rack. Using paper overhang, lift cake out of pan, and transfer to a cutting board; cut into 16 squares. (Brownies can be kept in an airtight container at room temperature up to 3 days.)

Whole-Wheat Fig Crumble Squares

This recipe features one batch of dough used for both the press-in crust and the streusel topping. The bars make perfect after-school snacks. Apple cider sweetens and moistens the fig filling. MAKES 16

1½ sticks (¾ cup) cold unsalted butter, cut into pieces, plus more for pan

1 cup plus 2 tablespoons all-purpose flour

1 cup whole-wheat flour

1 cup plus 2 tablespoons natural cane sugar

8 ounces dried Calimyrna figs (about 1½ cups), stemmed and halved

¾ cup pure apple cider

1 teaspoon finely grated lemon zest

Preheat oven to 375°F. Lightly butter an 8-inch square baking pan and line with parchment, leaving a 2-inch overhang on two sides. Butter parchment.

In a food processor, pulse together 1 cup all-purpose flour, the whole-wheat flour, and 1 cup sugar. Add butter and pulse until mixture resembles coarse meal. Transfer half of mixture to prepared pan; using lightly floured fingers, press firmly into bottom. Transfer remaining mixture to a bowl, and press into clumps.

In a clean food processor bowl, pulse together figs, apple cider, lemon zest, and remaining 2 tablespoons each all-purpose flour and sugar until a thick paste forms.

Using a small offset spatula or table knife, spread fig filling over crust. Sprinkle with topping. Bake, rotating pan halfway through, until topping is golden brown, 60 to 65 minutes.

Transfer pan to a wire rack and let cool completely. Using paper overhang, lift squares from pan, and transfer to a cutting board; cut into 16 squares. (Squares can be stored in an airtight container at room temperature up to 3 days.)

Spelt Honey-Cashew Blondies

We've taken butterscotch blondies to the next level: By replacing just a little bit of the brown sugar with honey and some of the butter with cashew butter, the flavor becomes complex and the texture is appealingly chewy. Since sprouted flour is less absorbent than other flours, it makes these blondies more moist, or "fudgy." MAKES 16

---

2 tablespoons unsalted butter, plus more for pan

¼ cup plus 2 tablespoons unsweetened cashew butter

¼ cup honey

¾ cup packed light brown sugar

1 large egg

1¼ cups sprouted spelt flour

½ teaspoon baking powder

¼ teaspoon coarse salt

1 ounce semisweet chocolate, coarsely chopped (¼ cup)

¼ cup coarsely chopped unsalted cashews

Preheat oven to 350°F. Lightly butter an 8-inch square baking pan and line with parchment, leaving a 2-inch overhang on two sides. Butter parchment.

In a saucepan over medium heat, melt butter with cashew butter and honey. Stir in brown sugar until combined. Remove from heat and let cool. Beat in egg, then flour, baking powder, and salt, stirring just until combined. Scrape batter into prepared pan. Smooth top; sprinkle with chopped chocolate and cashews.

Bake, rotating pan halfway through, until browned on edges and set, about 24 minutes. Transfer pan to a wire rack and let blondies cool completely. Using paper overhang, lift cake from pan and transfer to a cutting board; cut into 16 squares. (Blondies can be kept in an airtight container at room temperature up to 3 days.)

Vegan Lemon-Coconut Squares

Believe it or not, tofu works wonderfully in dessert: Combined with sugar and lemon, it provides the basis for an airy, ethereal egg-free lemon square. The whole-wheat crust is made with coconut oil instead of butter to keep the bars vegan. No need to wait for the crust to cool before adding the filling— because it contains no eggs, you can just pour it right in. MAKES 9

For the crust

- ½ cup virgin coconut oil, melted, plus more for pan
- ½ cup natural cane sugar
- 1 teaspoon vanilla extract
- ¼ teaspoon coarse salt
- 1½ cups whole-wheat pastry flour

For the filling

- ½ cup silken tofu
- ½ cup natural cane sugar
- 1 tablespoon grated lemon zest plus ½ cup fresh lemon juice (from 2 to 3 lemons)
- ½ teaspoon baking powder
- 2 tablespoons whole-wheat pastry flour

  Confectioners' sugar, for dusting

Make the crust: Preheat oven to 350°F. Lightly oil an 8-inch square baking dish, and line with parchment, leaving a 2-inch overhang on two sides. Oil parchment.

In a bowl, whisk together coconut oil, cane sugar, vanilla, and salt. Gradually add flour and stir until just combined. Press dough into prepared dish, and bake, rotating dish halfway through, until pale golden brown, about 20 minutes.

Meanwhile, make the filling: In a food processor, process tofu, cane sugar, lemon zest and juice, baking powder, and flour until smooth. Pour onto baked crust and bake, rotating pan halfway through, until set, 25 to 30 minutes. Transfer pan to a wire rack and let cake cool completely. Using paper overhang, lift cake from pan and transfer to a cutting board; dust with confectioners' sugar and cut into 9 squares. (Unsliced squares can be tightly wrapped and refrigerated up to 1 day; dust with confectioners' sugar and cut before serving.)

Cherry-Date Oat Bars

These nutty-sweet bars have a good amount of protein from almond butter and flaxseed meal. They make the ultimate snack for hikes. Free of refined sugar, the bars are sweetened with dried fruit, applesauce, and honey. MAKES 16

Virgin coconut oil or extra-virgin olive oil, for pan

3 cups old-fashioned rolled oats

¼ cup unsweetened dried cherries

¼ cup chopped pitted dates

2 teaspoons ground cinnamon

1 teaspoon coarse salt

¼ cup smooth natural unsalted almond butter, well-stirred, room temperature

¼ cup flaxseed meal (ground flaxseeds)

¼ cup unsweetened applesauce

⅓ cup honey

3 tablespoons fresh orange juice

¼ teaspoon vanilla extract

Preheat oven to 350°F. Lightly oil an 8-inch square baking dish, and line with parchment, leaving a 2-inch overhang on two sides. Oil parchment.

In a medium bowl, toss oats with cherries, dates, cinnamon, and salt.

In another bowl, stir almond butter with flaxseed meal, applesauce, honey, orange juice, and vanilla. Add almond butter mixture to oats mixture and stir to combine well.

Press mixture evenly into pan, using your fingers. Bake on middle rack, rotating pan halfway through, until golden brown and firm, 30 minutes. Transfer pan to a wire rack and let cool completely. Using paper overhang, lift cake from pan and transfer to a cutting board; cut into 16 squares. (Bars can be kept in an airtight container at room temperature up to 3 days.)

Sweet Oat-Walnut Crisps

Think of these as cracker-like cookies that are sweet enough to serve with afternoon tea but hearty enough to spread with cheese. The versatile, unassuming crisps were a surprise favorite in the Martha Stewart Living test kitchen. MAKES 2 DOZEN

1½ cups old-fashioned rolled oats

1 cup spelt flour

¼ cup plus 2 tablespoons packed light brown sugar

½ teaspoon baking soda

½ teaspoon coarse salt

½ cup finely chopped walnuts

¼ cup flaxseeds

1 stick (½ cup) cold unsalted butter, cut into small pieces

¼ cup cold sour cream

Soft cheese, for serving (optional)

Preheat oven to 350°F. In a bowl, toss together oats, flour, brown sugar, baking soda, salt, walnuts, and flaxseeds. Add butter and work in with your fingers or a pastry blender until pieces the size of small peas form. Stir in sour cream until combined.

Roll dough between two sheets of parchment into a 12½-by-12-inch rectangle, ⅛ inch thick. Using a sharp knife or a pizza wheel, cut dough into 4-by-1½-inch rectangles. Transfer dough to parchment-lined baking sheets, about ½ inch apart, and freeze 10 minutes.

Bake, rotating sheets halfway through, until crisp and golden along the edges, 12 to 14 minutes. Transfer baking sheets to wire racks and let crisps cool completely. Serve with cheese, if desired. (Crisps can be stored in an airtight container at room temperature up to 5 days.)

Fruit and Honey Nut Bars

Pureed dates and honey syrup bind and sweeten these chewy energy bars, which taste so much fresher than store-bought ones. Experiment with the ingredients: Feel free to swap the suggested nuts and dried fruits with others more to your liking. To make them vegan, use brown rice syrup in place of honey. MAKES 8

1 cup pitted dates

1 cup water

Safflower oil, for pan

1 cup pecans, toasted and coarsely chopped (see page 288)

½ cup unsalted macadamia nuts, toasted and coarsely chopped (see page 288)

1½ cups old-fashioned rolled oats, or 1 cup quinoa flakes

⅓ cup dried papaya, cut into ½-inch pieces

⅓ cup unsweetened dried cherries, chopped

⅓ cup unsweetened dried blueberries

2 tablespoons oat bran

3 tablespoons flaxseed meal (ground flaxseeds)

2 tablespoons toasted wheat germ

½ teaspoon coarse salt

½ teaspoon ground cinnamon

3 tablespoons honey

Preheat oven to 350°F. In a small saucepan, cover dates with water, and bring to a simmer; drain. Puree in a food processor until smooth.

Lightly oil an 8-inch square baking dish, and line with parchment, leaving a 2-inch overhang on two sides. Oil parchment.

In a food processor, pulse half the pecans and macadamia nuts until finely ground. In a large bowl, mix oats, ground and chopped nuts, dried fruits, oat bran, flaxseed meal, wheat germ, salt, and cinnamon. Stir in date puree and honey until combined. Press mixture evenly into pan using your fingers.

Bake, rotating pan halfway through, until center is firm and edges are golden, about 25 minutes. Transfer pan to a wire rack and let cool. Cut into 8 bars. (Bars can be kept in an airtight container at room temperature up to 5 days.)

Graham Crackers

Graham crackers are a favorite of kids and adults alike, especially when they're baked from scratch. Try them drizzled with melted chocolate, dusted with cardamom sugar, or sprinkled with flaky salt. (And don't forget s'mores, of course!) You can substitute whole-wheat flour for the graham flour. MAKES 30

1½ cups all-purpose flour, plus more for parchment

1 cup graham flour

½ cup toasted wheat germ

1 teaspoon ground cinnamon

¾ teaspoon baking soda

½ teaspoon coarse salt

2 sticks (1 cup) unsalted butter, room temperature

¾ cup packed light brown sugar

2 tablespoons honey

Variations

Melt 2 ounces bittersweet chocolate and transfer to a resealable plastic bag. Cut a tiny opening in 1 corner and drizzle the baked and cooled crackers with chocolate. Refrigerate until set.

To top crackers with spiced sugar, mix 2 tablespoons sugar and ½ teaspoon ground cardamom or ground cinnamon. Sprinkle over cut dough before baking.

For a salty-sweet cracker, top with ½ teaspoon flaky sea salt before baking.

In a bowl, whisk together both flours, wheat germ, cinnamon, baking soda, and salt. In another bowl, with an electric mixer, beat butter and brown sugar on medium until pale and fluffy, about 2 minutes. Beat in honey. Scrape down sides of bowl. With mixer on low, gradually add flour mixture, and beat just until combined.

Turn out dough and divide in half. Shape dough into 2 rectangles. Wrap each in plastic and refrigerate for 20 minutes. On a lightly floured piece of parchment, roll out each to a 12-by-10-inch rectangle, ⅛ to ¼ inch thick. Refrigerate until firm, about 30 minutes.

Preheat oven to 350°F. Using a fluted pie cutter, mark 24 rectangles (each about 2 by 4 inches) on each dough sheet, scoring but not cutting all the way through. Prick dough with a skewer or fork to create dotted lines. Freeze until firm, about 30 minutes.

Bake (still on parchment), rotating sheets halfway through, until golden brown, 17 to 19 minutes. Let cool on sheets. Break crackers at perforations. (Crackers can be kept in an airtight container at room temperature up to 1 week.)

Amaranth Clusters

Amaranth is a protein- and iron-rich grain. Here it's mixed with oats, nuts, and dried fruit. The mixture is bound together with honey and egg whites, formed into rounds, and baked until crisp. MAKES 18

1½ cups old-fashioned rolled oats

½ cup amaranth

½ cup macadamia nuts, toasted and finely chopped (see page 288)

½ cup dried cherries, coarsely chopped

½ cup dried apricots, coarsely chopped

¼ cup honey

2 large egg whites

¼ teaspoon coarse salt

In a bowl, combine oats, amaranth, macadamia nuts, dried fruits, and honey. Whisk egg whites with salt until foamy. Pour over dried fruit mixture, and stir to combine.

Preheat oven to 350°F. Scoop 3-tablespoon mounds of mixture, using an ice cream scoop, on parchment-lined baking sheets; pat into 3-inch rounds. Bake, rotating sheets halfway through, until clusters are golden brown, 15 to 18 minutes. Transfer to wire racks and let cool completely. (Clusters can be kept in an airtight container at room temperature up to 1 week.)

Pies, Tarts, Crisps, and Cobblers

Vegan Apple Pie

Spiced Pumpkin Pie with Crisp Rice Crust

Lattice-Topped Nectarine Pie

Ginger-Mango Cream Pie

Chocolate-Coconut Pie

Graham Flour and Jam Pastry Squares

Mixed-Berry Hand Pies

Kale and White Bean Hand Pies

Herb Quiche with Rye Crust

Plum Galette with Cornmeal Crust

Mushroom Tart

Butternut Squash Tart

Almond-Milk Custard Tart

Blueberry-Ricotta Tart

Pear Galette with Graham Crust

Strawberry-Cherry Whole Grain Crumble

Rhubarb and Raspberry Rye Crisp

Pear-Oat Crisps

Cinnamon-Apple Cranberry Crunch

Berry Cobbler with Cornmeal Biscuits

Vegan Apple Pie

We tested countless formulas to come up with the right combination of flours and fats to produce a stellar vegan pie. In the end, we preferred using an equal amount of spelt and all-purpose flours, and substituted safflower oil (which, unlike coconut oil or olive oil, adds no flavor) for butter or lard. The dough is easy to roll out and bakes into a crisp yet tender crust. MAKES ONE 9-INCH PIE

For the crust

1½ cups spelt flour

1½ cups all-purpose flour, plus more for dusting

2 tablespoons natural cane sugar

2 teaspoons coarse salt

½ cup safflower oil

½ cup water, plus more for brushing

For the filling

3 pounds assorted apples (about 6), such as Granny Smith, Gala, Empire, and Macoun, peeled, cored, and cut into ¼-inch slices

2 tablespoons fresh lemon juice

¼ cup natural cane sugar

1 teaspoon ground cinnamon

⅛ teaspoon coarse salt

3 tablespoons all-purpose flour

Raw sugar, such as turbinado, for sprinkling

Make the crust: In a bowl, whisk together both flours, sugar, and salt. Make a well in the center; add oil and the water, and knead until mixture comes together into a rough ball. Use your hands to mix until just combined. Divide dough into 2 balls, and loosely wrap each in plastic. Press with a rolling pin to form 2 disks. Let dough rest 30 minutes at room temperature.

Preheat oven to 400°F with rack in lower third. On a floured surface, roll out one disk to a 13-inch round, about ⅛ inch thick. Fit into a 9-inch pie dish. Trim edge flush with rim. Roll out second disk to a 13-inch round.

Make the filling: In a large bowl, toss together apples, lemon juice, cane sugar, cinnamon, salt, and flour. Transfer apples to pie shell; brush edge of dough with water, and top with second round. Tuck edges under bottom dough to seal; crimp as desired. Cut steam vents. Brush top with water and sprinkle with raw sugar.

Place pie dish on a rimmed baking sheet, and bake until crust begins to turn golden brown, 20 minutes. Reduce temperature to 350°F and bake, rotating halfway through, until browned on top and juices are bubbling in center, 60 to 70 minutes. Let cool completely on a wire rack before slicing and serving. (Pie is best the day it's made. Dough can be refrigerated up to 2 days.)

Spiced Pumpkin Pie with Crisp Rice Crust

Butter, brown sugar, and almonds are combined in this cookie-like crust. Rice cereal keeps it crisp (and gluten-free!). You can make this pie with homemade squash puree (see page 286 for recipe) or canned pumpkin puree. For an extra-delicious dessert, seek out muscovado sugar, an extraordinarily flavorful unrefined version of brown sugar. MAKES ONE 9-INCH PIE

For the crust

- 3 cups gluten-free rice-square cereal, such as Rice Chex
- ½ cup sliced almonds
- 5 tablespoons unsalted butter, melted
- ¼ cup plus 1 tablespoon packed light muscovado or light brown sugar
- ¼ teaspoon coarse salt

For the filling

- 1½ cups canned unsweetened pumpkin puree or Steamed Squash Puree (page 286)
- 3 large eggs, room temperature
- ¾ cup packed light muscovado or light brown sugar
- 1 tablespoon cornstarch
- ½ teaspoon coarse salt
- 1 teaspoon ground cinnamon
- ¼ teaspoon freshly grated nutmeg

  Pinch ground cloves
- 1 cup milk (½ cup, if using acorn-squash puree)

  Honey Whipped Yogurt
  (see page 195)

Make the crust: Preheat oven to 375°F. In a food processor, pulse cereal and almonds until finely ground. Add butter, brown sugar, and salt, and pulse until combined.

Press crust mixture evenly into bottom and up sides of a 9-inch pie dish. Bake until golden brown, about 12 minutes. Let cool completely. Reduce temperature to 325°F.

Make the filling: In a bowl, whisk together pumpkin puree and eggs. In another bowl, stir together brown sugar, cornstarch, salt, and spices; whisk in pumpkin mixture. Whisk in milk.

Place pie dish on a rimmed baking sheet. Pour filling into crust, and bake until filling is just set, 50 to 55 minutes. Let cool completely on a wire rack. Serve room temperature or chilled, with Honey Whipped Yogurt. (Pie can be refrigerated, covered, up to 2 days.)

Lattice-Topped Nectarine Pie

Of course, you can make a lattice-topped pie with any type of crust, but we think spelt's brown sugary sweetness is especially delicious with peaches and other luscious peak-of-summer fruits. To use peaches instead of nectarines, peel them first: Score the bottoms with an "X" and quickly blanch to remove fuzzy skins. MAKES ONE 9-INCH PIE

3 pounds nectarines (6 to 8), pitted and cut into ½-inch wedges

½ cup natural cane sugar

¼ cup cornstarch

1 tablespoon fresh lemon juice

¼ teaspoon coarse salt

All-purpose flour, for dusting

Spelt Pâte Brisée (recipe, page 138)

2 tablespoons unsalted butter, cut into small pieces

1 large egg, lightly beaten, for brushing

Raw sugar, such as turbinado, for sprinkling

In a large bowl, stir together nectarines, cane sugar, cornstarch, lemon juice, and salt.

On a lightly floured surface, roll out one disk of Spelt Pâte Brisée to a 13-inch round, about ⅛ inch thick. Fit dough into a 9-inch glass pie plate. Pour in filling and dot with butter; refrigerate.

On a lightly floured work surface, roll out remaining disk of dough ⅛ inch thick. Using a pastry wheel, cut seven 1½-inch strips from dough (see next page for how-to). Lay 3 strips across pie. Fold back every other strip and lay a perpendicular strip across the center of the pie. Unfold strips, then fold back remaining strip. Lay another strip across pie. Repeat folding and unfolding strips to weave a lattice pattern. Trim bottom and top crust to a 1-inch overhang, and press together to seal around edges. Fold edges under and crimp as desired. Refrigerate for 30 minutes.

Preheat oven to 400°F with rack in the lower third of oven. Brush lattice and edge with beaten egg, and sprinkle with turbinado sugar. Place pie on a parchment-lined baking sheet. Bake 20 minutes, then reduce oven temperature to 375°F. Bake, rotating sheet halfway through, until bottom crust is golden and filling is vigorously bubbling in center, about 70 minutes. (Loosely tent with foil if top is browning too quickly.) Transfer pie to a wire rack; let cool completely, at least 4 hours and up to overnight.

How to Make a Lattice Top

1 Roll out one disk of dough to a 13-inch round, about ⅛ inch thick. Using a pastry wheel, and a straight edge, cut seven 1½-inch-thick strips. **2** Lay 3 strips of dough across pie. **3** Fold back every other strip, and lay a strip across the center of the pie, perpendicular to others. **4** Unfold strips.

5 Fold back remaining strip and lay another strip across the pie. 6 Repeat folding and unfolding strips to weave a lattice pattern. 7 Trim bottom and top crust to a 1-inch overhang, and press to seal around edges. 8 Fold edges under and crimp as desired. Refrigerate until firm, 30 minutes, before baking.

Spelt Pâte Brisée

We like the combination of spelt and all-purpose flours: The spelt adds its characteristic maple flavor and tender texture, while the all-purpose provides structure. The keys to a flaky crust are starting with well-chilled ingredients and adequately chilling the dough before rolling it out.

1¼ cups spelt flour

1¼ cups all-purpose flour

1 tablespoon natural cane sugar

2 teaspoons coarse salt

2 sticks (1 cup) cold unsalted butter, cut into small pieces

6 to 8 tablespoons ice water

In a food processor, pulse flours, granulated sugar, and salt until combined. (Alternatively, see How to Make Pie Dough by Hand, page 140.) Add butter and pulse until mixture resembles coarse meal, with a few pea-size pieces remaining. Evenly drizzle with 6 tablespoons ice water. Pulse just until dough is crumbly but holds together when squeezed, adding more water as needed (do not overmix).

Halve dough and turn out onto 2 sheets of plastic wrap. Form into 2 disks. Wrap in the plastic and refrigerate until firm, at least 1 hour and up to overnight. (Dough can be frozen up to 1 month; thaw overnight in refrigerator before using.)

How to Make Pie Dough By Hand

<u>1</u> Have everything—ingredients and equipment—measured and chilled. <u>2</u> Cut cold, cubed butter into dry ingredients with a pastry blender. <u>3</u> After cutting in butter, the mixture should resemble coarse meal with a few pea-size pieces remaining. <u>4</u> Drizzle in water and gently mix in with pastry blender or a fork.

5 Stop mixing when dough holds together in large clumps when squeezed (do not overmix). **6** Turn out dough (it will be crumbly) onto two pieces of plastic wrap. **7** Using your knuckles, press down on each piece of dough to bring it together. **8** Using a rolling pin, form dough into disks; wrap tightly in plastic.

Ginger-Mango Cream Pie

In this pie, the favorite breakfast combo—yogurt and granola—becomes dessert worthy. The granola is used in place of cookies as the base for a press-in crust. For the no-bake filling, cream cheese and Greek yogurt get beaten together and sweetened with honey; grated fresh ginger is a nice match for sweet mango. MAKES ONE 9-INCH PIE

1½ cups plain granola (without dried fruit)

3 tablespoons natural cane sugar

4 tablespoons unsalted butter, melted

8 ounces cream cheese, room temperature

¾ cup Greek yogurt

2 tablespoons honey, plus more for drizzling

1 teaspoon grated fresh ginger

1 mango, peeled

Preheat oven to 375°F. In a food processor, pulse granola and sugar until finely chopped. Drizzle butter over granola mixture and pulse to combine. Press mixture into and up sides of a 9-inch pie dish. Bake until golden, about 10 minutes. Transfer to a wire rack and let cool.

With an electric mixer, beat cream cheese on medium until smooth, about 1 minute. Add yogurt, 2 tablespoons honey, and ginger and beat until combined.

Pour filling into prepared crust and smooth top. Chill in refrigerator until set, at least 6 hours and up to 1 day.

Cut mango flesh away from pit and thinly slice. Just before serving, arrange mango on top of pie and drizzle with honey.

Chocolate-Coconut Pie

Set in a graham cracker crust, the filling for this creamy chocolate pie involves folding a luscious ganache into a marshmallowy Italian meringue. Instead of heavy cream, the ganache relies on coconut milk, and the crust calls for coconut oil in place of butter. The result is a dairy-free take (assuming your crackers are dairy-free) on chocolate cream pie, with a sprinkling of cocoa nibs for extra chocolate punch. MAKES ONE 9-INCH PIE

For the crust

- 12 graham crackers (6½ ounces)
- ¼ cup melted virgin coconut oil
- 2 tablespoons water
- 3 tablespoons natural cane sugar
- ¼ teaspoon coarse salt

For the filling

- 8 ounces unsweetened chocolate, finely chopped
- 1 can (14 ounces) unsweetened coconut milk
- ½ cup natural cane sugar
- ¼ cup water
- 2 large egg whites, room temperature
- ½ teaspoon vanilla extract
- Cocoa nibs, for garnish

Make the crust: Preheat oven to 350°F. In a food processor, pulse graham crackers until finely ground (you should have 1½ cups). Add oil, the water, sugar, and salt and pulse until combined. Firmly press crumb into bottom and up sides of a 9-inch pie dish. Bake until crust is fragrant and edges are golden, 12 to 14 minutes. Transfer to a wire rack and let cool completely.

Make the filling: Set chopped chocolate in a heatproof bowl. In a small saucepan, bring coconut milk just to a boil. Pour milk over chocolate and let stand 2 minutes; then stir with a flexible spatula until ganache is thick and glossy. Let cool to room temperature, stirring occasionally.

In a small saucepan, combine sugar and water and brush sides of pot with a wet pastry brush to remove sugar crystals. Bring to a boil, stirring occasionally until sugar is dissolved. Meanwhile, using a stand mixer, whisk egg whites and vanilla on medium. Continue cooking sugar, without stirring, until it reaches 238°F on a candy thermometer. With the mixer running, carefully pour hot sugar in a slow, steady stream into egg whites. Increase speed to high, and whisk until stiff peaks form, 1 minute.

Pour ganache into meringue and gently fold, leaving some streaks, if desired. Pour into cooled crust and sprinkle with cocoa nibs. Refrigerate until firm, at least 1 hour and up to 1 day.

5 Thickeners for Fruit Desserts

Starches are the secret to properly thickening the juices in baked fruit desserts (as well as to creating stable custards). Here are a few things to consider when using thickeners, including the pros and cons of each available option.

1 All-purpose flour

This widely available starch works best in desserts with neutral-colored fruits, like apples and pears, or acidic ingredients, like rhubarb; it can make more vibrantly colored fillings look cloudy. Of the five starches here, flour is the only one that contains gluten. Flour is half as powerful as cornstarch, so you'll need to use double when substituting.

2 Arrowroot powder

Derived from a tuber, arrowroot powder has become a favorite thickener of new-school pie bakers because it has a neutral flavor. It works well with acidic ingredients, like rhubarb and sour cherries, and creates clear, jewel-like juices without the same chewy quality of tapioca. Arrowroot should not be used with dairy-based fillings because it compromises the texture. When substituting arrowroot for cornstarch, use one and a half times as much arrowroot as you would cornstarch.

3 Cornstarch

Because it's so accessible and sturdy, cornstarch is our thickener of choice in most fruit fillings, as long as they are not too acidic. We also like it for custards because it can withstand longer direct heat (unlike tapioca) and pairs well with dairy (unlike arrowroot). When too much cornstarch is used, it can make fruit fillings appear cloudy and seem gummy.

4 Potato starch

Not to be confused with potato flour, potato starch is often the thickener of choice in Europe. In the United States, it's sometimes used as a substitute for cornstarch because it's kosher for Passover. Potato starch creates a thick, high-gloss filling that can seem gluey if used in excess. Use half as much potato starch as you would cornstarch.

5 Tapioca

Derived from the cassava tuber, tapioca is available as small granules, known as pearl tapioca, as well as finely ground tapioca starch. Whether you use the starch or the granules (which don't completely dissolve), tapioca creates fillings with a clear, jelly-like quality and slightly chewy texture. Use it in pies you plan to freeze and reheat; the juices are less likely to weep through the crust when thawed. You can substitute tapioca starch one-for-one with cornstarch.

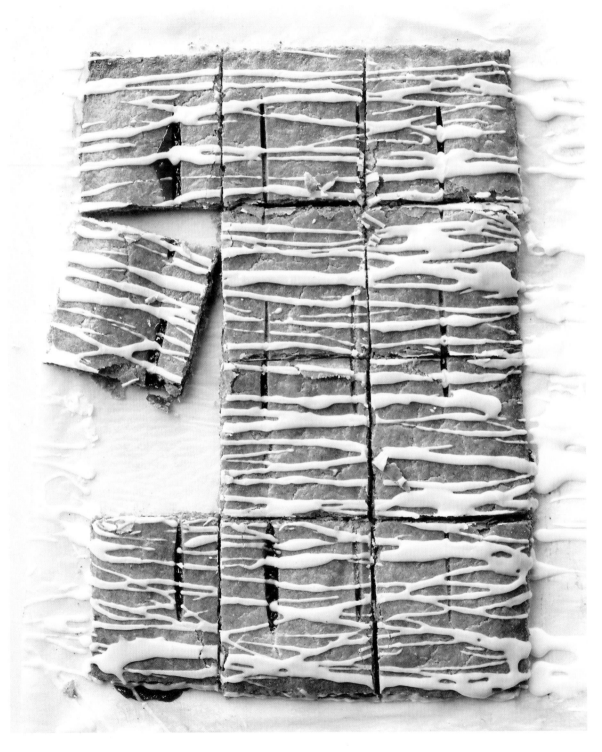

Graham Flour and Jam Pastry Squares

If you're a fan of toaster pastries, wait until you taste this homemade version. (The squares are a great option for bake sales.) Graham flour adds a satisfying heartiness to the rich pastry. MAKES 1 DOZEN

1¼ cups all-purpose flour, plus more for dusting

1¼ cups whole-wheat graham flour

1½ teaspoons coarse salt

1 stick (½ cup) cold unsalted butter, cut into cubes

4 ounces cold cream cheese, cut into cubes

½ cup plus 1 tablespoon ice water

1 cup raspberry jam

1 large egg, lightly beaten

½ recipe Drizzly Glaze, page 287

In a food processor, pulse both flours and the salt to combine. Add butter and cream cheese, and pulse until small pieces remain. Add ice water and pulse until dough just starts to clump together.

Turn out dough (it will be crumbly) onto a clean surface and divide in half. Wrap each half in plastic wrap and press to form a rectangle. Refrigerate dough until firm, at least 20 minutes and up to 1 day.

On lightly floured parchment, roll out each piece of dough to a 10-by-14½-inch rectangle. Transfer one rectangle with parchment to a baking sheet. Spread jam on top, leaving a 1-inch border. Roll up remaining rectangle on rolling pin, then unroll on top of first rectangle. Press edges together, then use a crimped pastry wheel to trim all around. Brush beaten egg over top, then use a paring knife to cut a few vents in top crust. Refrigerate 30 minutes.

Preheat oven to 375°F. Bake, rotating sheet halfway through, until pastry is golden and jam is bubbling, 35 minutes. Transfer sheet to a wire rack and let pastry cool.

Drizzle glaze over pastry, then let set at least 10 minutes before cutting into 12 squares. (Unglazed pastry can be stored at room temperature, covered in plastic, up to 1 day.)

Mixed-Berry Hand Pies

With a lightly sweet filling and spelt crust, these hand pies taste wholesome enough to eat for breakfast as well as dessert. If you can't find tasty fresh berries, use thawed frozen berries, preferably organic. MAKES 12

2 cups fresh raspberries (10 ounces)

2 cups fresh blueberries (12 ounces)

½ cup packed light brown sugar

¼ cup plus 2 tablespoons cornstarch

Pinch coarse salt

All-purpose flour, for dusting

Spelt Pâte Brisée (see page 138)

1 large egg, lightly beaten

Raw sugar, such as turbinado, for sprinkling

In a large bowl, gently stir together berries, brown sugar, cornstarch, and salt.

On a lightly floured work surface, roll out one piece of dough to a 15½-by-10½-inch rectangle (see next page for how-to). Using a sharp knife or pastry wheel, trim to 15 by 10 inches. Cut into six 5-inch squares. Using a dry pastry brush, sweep off excess flour. Working with one square at a time, place 2 tablespoons filling in center. Brush two connecting edges with beaten egg and fold over filling to form a triangle; press to seal. Fill and fold with remaining dough and filling. Transfer pies to a parchment-lined baking sheet. Refrigerate pies for at least 20 minutes and up to 1 hour.

Preheat oven to 375°F. Using a paring knife, cut a few steam vents in the center of each hand pie. Brush pies with remaining egg and sprinkle with raw sugar. Bake, rotating sheet halfway through, until crusts are golden brown and filling is bubbling, 25 to 30 minutes. Transfer sheet to a wire rack and let pies cool slightly. Serve warm or at room temperature. (Unbaked hand pies can be tightly wrapped and frozen up to 1 month. Bake from frozen.)

How to Assemble Hand Pies

<u>1</u> On a lightly floured work surface, roll out each piece of dough to a 15½-by-10½-inch rectangle. Trim to 15 by 10 inches. <u>2</u> Cut each into six 5-inch squares. <u>3</u> Place filling in center of each square. <u>4</u> Brush two connecting edges with beaten egg and fold over filling to form triangles; press to seal.

Brush hand pies with remaining egg and sprinkle with raw sugar. Cut a few steam vents in the center of each hand pie before baking.

Kale and White Bean Hand Pies

These portable pastries are terrific for picnics and on-the-go lunches. MAKES 12

For the crust

- 1¾ cups all-purpose flour, plus more for dusting
- ¾ cup rye flour
- ½ cup finely grated pecorino Romano cheese
- ¾ teaspoon coarse salt
- 2 sticks (1 cup) cold unsalted butter, cut into small pieces
- 6 to 8 tablespoons ice water

For the filling

- 2 tablespoons unsalted butter
- 1 small yellow onion, diced
- 1 teaspoon fresh thyme leaves
- 1 bunch kale (8 ounces), tough stems discarded, leaves coarsely chopped
- Coarse salt and ground pepper
- 1 can (14.5 ounces) cannellini beans, preferably low-sodium, rinsed and drained
- 2 tablespoons all-purpose flour
- 1 cup low-sodium chicken or vegetable broth
- 1 large egg, lightly beaten

Make the crust: In a food processor, pulse both flours, cheese, and salt to combine. Add butter; pulse until mixture resembles coarse meal, with a few pea-size pieces of butter. Sprinkle with 6 tablespoons ice water. Pulse until dough just holds together; add up to 2 more tablespoons water, gradually adding, if necessary. Halve dough, and form into two 1-inch-thick rectangles, wrap in plastic, and refrigerate 1 hour or up to 3 days.

Make the pies: In a skillet, melt butter over medium-high heat. Add onion and thyme, and cook, stirring, until softened, 3 minutes. Add kale, season with salt and pepper, and cook until kale wilts, 2 minutes. Add beans and cook 2 minutes. Stir in 2 tablespoons flour. Add broth and bring to a boil, cook, stirring until thickened, 2 minutes. Transfer to a bowl, and season with salt and pepper. Let cool completely.

Preheat oven to 400°F. On a lightly floured surface, roll out one piece of dough to a 15½-by-10½-inch rectangle. Trim to 15 by 10 inches. Cut into six 5-inch squares. Brush off excess flour. Working with one square at a time, place about ¼ cup of filling in center. Brush edges on half of the square with egg and fold dough over filling to form a rectangle; seal edges with a fork. Transfer to a parchment-lined baking sheet. Fill and fold remaining dough and filling; refrigerate pies for 20 minutes and up to 1 hour.

Cut a few steam vents in center of each pie. Brush tops with egg. Bake, rotating sheet halfway through, until golden brown, 20 to 30 minutes. Let pies cool on a wire rack. Serve warm or at room temperature.

Herb Quiche with Rye Crust

The custardy filling for this quiche is simple, to allow the flavor of the rye-fennel seed crust to come through (we like caraway seeds here, too). You can add 1 cup of briefly sautéed or blanched vegetables, such as broccoli, asparagus, or greens, to the quiche. Just be sure not to overfill the crust with the custard mixture; it should reach just to the top of the crust. MAKES ONE 9-INCH QUICHE

For the crust

- ½ cup rye flour
- ¾ cup all-purpose flour, plus more for dusting
- ½ teaspoon coarse salt
- ½ teaspoon fennel or caraway seeds
- 1 stick (½ cup) cold unsalted butter, cut into small pieces
- 3 to 4 tablespoons ice water

For the filling

- 3 large eggs
- ¾ cup heavy cream
- ¾ cup milk
- ¾ teaspoon coarse salt
- ¼ teaspoon freshly ground pepper
- ½ cup packed small fresh herb sprigs, such as chervil and dill

Make the crust: In a food processor, pulse flours, salt, and seeds to combine. (Alternatively, see How to Make Pie Dough by Hand, page 140.) Add butter and pulse until mixture resembles coarse meal. Drizzle with 3 tablespoons ice water. Pulse until dough is crumbly but just holds together; if necessary, add up to 1 tablespoon more water. Transfer dough to a piece of plastic wrap and form into a disk. Wrap and refrigerate at least 1 hour and up to overnight.

On a floured surface, roll out dough to a 13-inch round, ⅛ inch thick. Fit into a 9-inch pie plate. Fold edges of dough under and crimp. Freeze 30 minutes.

Preheat oven 400°F. Line shell with parchment; fill with pie weights or dried beans. Transfer pie plate to a rimmed baking sheet and bake 20 minutes. Remove paper and beans. Bake until golden, 10 to 12 minutes. Transfer to a wire rack and let crust cool completely.

Make the filling: Reduce oven to 375°F. In a bowl, whisk together eggs, cream, milk, salt, and pepper. Set pie plate on a rimmed baking sheet and pour custard into cooled crust, stopping just short of top.

Arrange herb sprigs on top. Bake 10 minutes. Reduce temperature to 325°F. Continue baking, rotating sheet halfway through, until golden and set, about 55 minutes. Transfer quiche to wire rack and let cool at least 1 hour before serving.

Plum Galette with Cornmeal Crust

The buttery cornmeal crust perfectly balances a tart-sweet filling. Look for red, black, golden, or Shiro plums at the farmers' market. MAKES ONE 8-INCH GALETTE

For the crust

- 1 cup all-purpose flour, plus more for dusting
- ¼ cup fine cornmeal
- 1 tablespoon natural cane sugar
- ½ teaspoon coarse salt
- 1 stick (½ cup) cold unsalted butter, cut into small pieces
- 1 large egg yolk
- 2 to 4 tablespoons ice water

For the filling

- ¼ cup natural cane sugar
- 1 vanilla bean, split and seeds scraped
- 2 tablespoons cornstarch
- 1¼ pounds small plums, pitted and sliced into ½-inch wedges
- 1 tablespoon unsalted butter, cut into pieces
- 1 large egg lightly beaten with 1 teaspoon water
- Raw sugar, such as turbinado, for sprinkling

Make the crust: In a food processor, combine flour, cornmeal, cane sugar, and salt. Add butter and pulse just until mixture resembles coarse meal.

In a bowl, lightly beat egg yolk; add 2 tablespoons ice water. With machine running, add egg yolk mixture in a slow, steady stream. Pulse until dough just holds together; add up to 2 tablespoons more water, 1 tablespoon at a time, if necessary. Gather dough into a ball and flatten into a disk. Wrap in plastic. Refrigerate at least 1 hour and up to overnight.

Make the filling: In a bowl, stir together cane sugar and vanilla seeds; stir in cornstarch. Add plums and toss until coated. On lightly floured parchment, roll out dough to a 12-inch round, ¼ to ⅛ inch thick. Transfer dough and parchment to a baking sheet. Arrange plums in center of dough, leaving a 2-inch border. Fold border over filling, overlapping slightly and pressing to adhere folds. Dot butter over filling. Refrigerate until firm, about 30 minutes.

Preheat oven to 375°F. Brush edges of dough with egg wash and sprinkle with raw sugar. Bake, rotating sheet halfway through, until crust is golden brown and juices are bubbling, 45 minutes. Transfer baking sheet to a wire rack and let galette cool. Serve warm or at room temperature. (Galette is best the day it's made. Dough can be frozen up to 1 month; thaw overnight in refrigerator before using.)

Mushroom Tart

A mushroom filling is made more savory with a generous amount of grated Gruyère. You can use any mushroom you like, but a mix of varieties—including oyster, shiitake, and hen of the woods—is especially flavorful and eye-catching. The whole-wheat and olive oil crust is based on a recipe for crackers. The real surprise here is the addition of tahini—toasted sesame paste—in the crust; it makes the whole tart taste more complex. MAKES ONE 9½-INCH TART

For the crust

- ¾ cup whole-wheat flour
- ¾ cup all-purpose flour, plus more for dusting
- 1 teaspoon coarse salt
- ¼ cup tahini
- 3 tablespoons extra-virgin olive oil
- 3 to 4 tablespoons ice water

For the filling

- 2 tablespoon extra-virgin olive oil
- ½ cup finely chopped shallot
- 1 garlic clove, minced
- ¼ teaspoon red-pepper flakes, plus more for serving
- 1 pound wild mushrooms, stems trimmed and caps sliced
- ½ teaspoon coarse salt
- ¾ cup coarsely grated Gruyère
- 2 large eggs, lightly beaten
- ¼ cup finely chopped flat-leaf fresh parsley leaves, plus more for serving

Make the crust: Preheat oven to 425°F. In a large bowl, whisk together both flours and salt. Stir in tahini, oil, and 3 tablespoons water. Knead in bowl until a ball forms; add up to 1 tablespoon more water, if needed. Transfer dough to a lightly floured surface. Roll dough into a 12-inch round and fit it into a 9½-inch tart pan with a removable bottom. Trim flush with rim. Prick bottom of dough all over with a fork. Bake, rotating pan halfway through, until crust is golden brown and crisp, about 35 minutes. Let cool on a wire rack.

Make the filling: Reduce oven temperature to 350°F. In a large skillet, heat oil over medium. Add shallot, garlic, and red-pepper flakes; cook, stirring, until shallot is softened, about 4 minutes. Add mushrooms and salt. Cook until mushrooms are tender and golden brown in spots, 6 to 8 minutes. Let cool slightly.

In a large bowl, combine cheese, eggs, parsley, and mushroom mixture. Pour filling into crust. Bake tart, rotating pan halfway through, until just set, 30 to 35 minutes. Transfer pan to a wire rack and let tart cool slightly, about 10 minutes. Top with parsley, and serve warm or at room temperature with more red-pepper flakes. (Tart can be refrigerated, covered, overnight; bring to room temperature or reheat before serving.)

Butternut Squash Tart

Roasted butternut squash makes a nice change from pumpkin in this not-so-sweet tart, perfect for your "I'm not big on dessert" friends. The wheat germ–spiked crust has only one quarter of the butter that's in a traditional pie dough, yet it is still flaky and tender, thanks to the buttermilk.

MAKES ONE 5-BY-11-INCH TART

For the crust

- 1¼ cups all-purpose flour, plus more for dusting
- 2 tablespoons toasted wheat germ
- 1 teaspoon natural cane sugar
- ¼ teaspoon coarse salt
- ½ teaspoon baking powder
- 4 tablespoons cold unsalted butter, cut into pieces
- ⅓ cup buttermilk

For the filling

- 1 butternut squash (1¾ pounds), peeled, halved, seeds removed, flesh cut crosswise ½ inch thick
- 2 teaspoons safflower oil
- ¼ cup plus 2 tablespoons packed light brown sugar
- ½ cup plus 2 teaspoons sliced almonds, toasted (see page 288)
- ¼ teaspoon coarse salt
- 1 large egg
- ½ teaspoon vanilla extract
- 1 tablespoon all-purpose flour
- Water, for brushing
- 1 teaspoon raw sugar, such as turbinado

Make the crust: In a food processor, pulse flour, wheat germ, cane sugar, salt, and baking powder. Add butter and pulse until the largest pieces are the size of peas. Add buttermilk and pulse until dough just holds together. Wrap in plastic and pat into a rectangle. Refrigerate at least 1 hour and up to overnight.

Make the filling: Preheat oven to 450°F. On a baking sheet, toss squash with oil and 2 tablespoons brown sugar. Roast until golden and tender, 15 minutes. Remove from oven and reduce temperature to 400°F.

In a food processor, pulse ½ cup almonds until finely ground. In a bowl, stir together remaining ¼ cup brown sugar, the ground almonds, salt, egg, vanilla, and flour.

On a lightly floured piece of parchment, roll out dough to a 9-by-15-inch rectangle and transfer to a baking sheet. Spread almond mixture on top, leaving a 2-inch border. Top with squash. Fold dough up and over each side. Lightly brush edges with water and sprinkle with raw sugar. Chill until firm, 30 minutes.

Bake, rotating sheet halfway through, until crust is golden brown, 25 to 30 minutes. Transfer sheet to a wire rack and let tart cool slightly. Sprinkle with remaining 2 teaspoons almonds. (Tart is best the day it's baked.)

Almond-Milk Custard Tart

The dairy-free custard in this almond milk tart is delicately creamy. In winter and early spring, oranges are lovely on top, but in summer you could also serve this topped with sliced ripe peaches or plump blackberries. MAKES ONE 9½-INCH TART

For the crust

- 1 cup sliced almonds
- ¼ cup natural cane sugar
- ¼ teaspoon coarse salt
- 1 cup all-purpose flour
- ¼ cup melted virgin coconut oil
- 1 to 2 tablespoons ice water

For the filling

- 4 large egg yolks
- ½ cup natural cane sugar
- ½ teaspoon finely grated orange zest
- ¼ cup cornstarch
- Pinch coarse salt
- 2 cups unsweetened almond milk, homemade (see page 282) or store-bought
- Peeled and sliced blood oranges, for serving
- Caramel Drizzle (page 287), for serving

Filled pie without oranges can be refrigerated, covered, overnight.

Make the crust: In a food processor, pulse almonds, sugar, and salt until finely ground. Add flour and pulse. With machine running, add oil and 1 tablespoon water in a steady stream, until dough just holds together. If crumbly, add up to 1 tablespoon more water. Transfer dough to a 9½-inch tart pan with a removable bottom. Press into bottom and up sides of pan. Cover and chill crust for at least 30 minutes.

Preheat oven to 375°F. Place parchment over crust, and fill with pie weights or dried beans. Bake until crust feels dry, 20 minutes. Remove parchment and weights; bake until crust is light golden brown, 8 to 10 minutes. Transfer pan to a wire rack and let cool completely.

Make the filling: With an electric mixer, beat egg yolks, sugar, and zest on medium until pale and thick, 2 to 3 minutes. Beat in cornstarch and salt.

In a saucepan, bring almond milk just to a boil. Whisking constantly, gradually add milk to egg mixture; then return to saucepan. Bring to a boil, whisking constantly until custard is thickened and coats the back of a spoon, 2 to 3 minutes.

Using a rubber spatula, press custard through a sieve into crust. Cover surface directly with plastic wrap and refrigerate until well chilled, about 2 hours. Just before serving, arrange oranges on top and drizzle with caramel.

Blueberry-Ricotta Tart

This tart strikes the right balance between healthy and indulgent. Here, ricotta is blended with just a touch of honey until creamy, then spread into a wheat germ–almond crust and crowned with lightly sweetened blueberries. (To make your own ricotta, see page 285.) If you'd like to add some whole-grain goodness, swap spelt flour for half the all-purpose. MAKES ONE 9-INCH TART

1 cup all-purpose flour, plus more for dusting

¼ cup finely ground blanched almonds or almond flour

2 tablespoons toasted wheat germ

2 tablespoons light brown sugar

½ teaspoon baking powder

¾ teaspoon coarse salt

4 tablespoons cold unsalted butter, cut into pieces

⅓ cup buttermilk

1¼ cups ricotta

¼ teaspoon ground cinnamon

3 tablespoons honey

1 pint fresh blueberries (2 cups)

For the freshest berries, look for those that are plump, deep blue, and have a mild, chalky coating called bloom— it's a sign of less handling.

In a food processor, pulse together flour, ground almonds, wheat germ, brown sugar, baking powder, and ½ teaspoon salt. (Or whisk together by hand in a bowl.) Add butter and pulse (or quickly cut in with a pastry blender or your fingertips) until largest pieces are the size of small peas. Add buttermilk and pulse (or mix with a fork) until dough just holds together. Pat into a disk, wrap in plastic, and refrigerate at least 1 hour and up to overnight.

Preheat oven to 375°F. On a lightly floured work surface, roll out dough to a 12-inch round, ⅛ inch thick. Fit into a 9-inch tart pan with a removable bottom. Trim edges flush with pan, and prick holes all over dough with fork. Freeze 15 minutes. Line with parchment, and fill with pie weights or dried beans. Bake until set, 25 minutes. Remove parchment and weights, and bake until golden brown and dry, 15 to 20 minutes more. Transfer pan to a wire rack and let shell cool completely.

In a food processor or blender, puree ricotta with remaining ¼ teaspoon salt, the cinnamon, and 1 tablespoon honey. Spread evenly into cooled shell. Refrigerate until well chilled, about 2 hours. Just before serving gently toss blueberries with remaining 2 tablespoons honey and arrange on top of tart. (Filled tart without berries can be refrigerated, covered, overnight.)

Pear Galette with Graham Crust

Coarsely ground graham flour lends a honeyed flavor to this crust, which brings out the vanilla in the pear filling. Red-skinned Bartlett pears look especially beautiful here, but if you cannot find them, green Bartlett or Bosc pears work equally well. MAKES ONE 9-INCH GALETTE

For the crust

- ½ cup plus 2 tablespoons graham flour
- ½ cup plus 2 tablespoons all-purpose flour, plus more for dusting
- ¾ teaspoon coarse salt
- ½ teaspoon natural cane sugar
- 1 stick (½ cup) cold unsalted butter, cut into small pieces
- 2 to 4 tablespoons ice water

For the filling

- ¼ cup natural cane sugar
- 1 tablespoon all-purpose flour
- 1 vanilla bean, split and seeds scraped
- 2 pounds Red Bartlett pears, halved lengthwise, cored, and sliced into ½-inch wedges
- 1 tablespoon unsalted butter, cut into small pieces
- 1 large egg, lightly beaten with 1 teaspoon water
  Raw sugar, such as turbinado, for sprinkling

Make the crust: In a food processor, pulse flours, salt, and cane sugar until combined. Add butter, and pulse until mixture resembles coarse meal with a few pea-size pieces of butter remaining. Sprinkle with 2 tablespoons ice water. Pulse until dough is crumbly but holds together when squeezed; add up to 2 tablespoons more, if necessary. Turn dough out on a large piece of plastic wrap. Fold plastic wrap over dough; press to shape into a 1-inch-thick disk. Refrigerate until firm, at least 1 hour or up to 3 days.

Make the filling: In a large bowl, stir together cane sugar, flour, and vanilla seeds. Add pears and toss to coat. On a lightly floured parchment, roll out dough to a 13-inch round, about ⅛ inch thick. Transfer parchment and dough to a rimmed baking sheet, and refrigerate until ready to use, up to overnight. Arrange fruit in the center of dough, leaving a 3-inch border. Fold border over pears, overlapping slightly and pressing to adhere folds. Dot butter over filling and refrigerate for 30 minutes.

Preheat oven to 400°F with rack in the lower third. Brush edges of dough with egg wash and sprinkle with raw sugar. Bake, rotating sheet halfway through, until crust is golden and fruit is bubbling, 1 hour. Transfer sheet to a wire rack and let galette cool. Serve warm or at room temperature.

Strawberry-Cherry Whole-Grain Crumble

It's best to serve this golden crumble in early summer, just as strawberry season gives way to cherry season. Chock-full of oats and unsweetened coconut flakes, with whole-wheat flour and coconut oil holding everything together, the wholesome topping also happens to be vegan. SERVES 6

For the crumble topping

⅓ cup whole-wheat flour

⅓ cup old-fashioned rolled oats

¼ cup large unsweetened coconut flakes

¼ cup packed light brown sugar

¼ teaspoon coarse salt

¼ cup virgin coconut oil

For the filling

8 ounces fresh strawberries, hulled and cut into ½-inch pieces (1½ cups)

8 ounces fresh sweet cherries, pitted and halved (1½ cups)

2 tablespoons packed light brown sugar

Make the crumble topping: Preheat oven to 350°F. In a medium bowl, combine flour, oats, coconut flakes, brown sugar, salt, and oil. Knead until oil is combined and mixture forms large crumbs.

Make the filling: In another bowl, toss strawberries and cherries with sugar.

Transfer filling to 9-inch pie dish. Top evenly with crumble topping. Bake, rotating dish halfway through, until topping is golden and filling is bubbling in center, 35 to 40 minutes. Let cool slightly before serving. (Crumble is best the day it's made.)

Rhubarb and Raspberry Rye Crisp

Rye flour adds a bold flavor to this crisp topping while taming the delightful tartness of the rhubarb. Although rhubarb is often associated with spring and strawberries, it grows prolifically in cool climates well into the summer, when raspberries are also in season. If you prefer, you can use an equal amount of strawberries. SERVES 6

1½ pounds rhubarb, cut into 1-inch pieces (about 4 cups)

½ pint fresh or thawed frozen raspberries

⅔ cup natural cane sugar

½ cup plus 2 tablespoons all-purpose flour

1 teaspoon finely grated orange zest plus juice of 1 orange

½ cup rye flour

½ cup packed dark brown sugar

½ teaspoon ground cinnamon

1 stick (½ cup) cold unsalted butter, cut into small pieces

½ cup old-fashioned rolled oats

¼ cup hazelnuts, toasted, skinned, and coarsely chopped (optional, see page 288)

Ice cream, for serving (optional)

Preheat oven to 350°F. In a large bowl, stir together rhubarb, raspberries, cane sugar, 2 tablespoons all-purpose flour, and the orange zest and juice.

In another bowl, combine the remaining ½ cup all-purpose flour, the rye flour, brown sugar, and cinnamon. Rub butter into flour mixture using your fingers or a pastry blender until it is well incorporated and large crumbs form. Stir in oats and nuts.

Turn rhubarb filling into a 9-inch square baking dish (or other 1½-quart baking dish), and cover with topping. Bake, rotating dish halfway through, until topping is browned and crisp and juices are bubbling in the center, about 45 minutes. Let cool slightly before serving with ice cream, if desired. (Crisp is best served the day it's made.)

Pear-Oat Crisps

Grab a canister of gluten-free rolled oats to make this crisp topping: Grind half the oats and keep the other half whole for the buttery crumbs. For even more texture, add some pumpkin seeds or chopped nuts to the mix. You can also make this crisp with peeled sliced peaches. SERVES 4 TO 6

For the topping

- 2 cups old-fashioned rolled oats
- ½ cup packed light brown sugar
- ¼ teaspoon coarse salt
- 1 stick (½ cup) unsalted butter, melted

For the filling

- 2 pounds pears, such as Bosc, peeled, cored, and cut into ½-inch slices
- ¼ cup dried unsweetened cherries
- 2 tablespoons packed light brown sugar
- ¼ teaspoon ground cinnamon

Make the topping: Preheat oven to 375°F. In a food processor, pulse 1 cup oats until coarsely ground. Transfer to a bowl, and add remaining 1 cup oats, the brown sugar, salt, and melted butter. Stir mixture until combined.

Make the filling: In a large bowl, toss together pears, cherries, brown sugar, and cinnamon until combined. Transfer to 4 shallow 5-inch round ramekins or one 9-inch-square baking dish. Sprinkle evenly with topping. Bake, rotating ramekins halfway through, until pears are tender and topping is golden brown, about 20 minutes for ramekins and 50 minutes for baking dish. Let cool slightly before serving. (Crisps are best served the day they're made.)

Cinnamon-Apple Cranberry Crunch

Crumpled sheets of phyllo dough stand in for the usual biscuit topping in this take on fruit cobbler. Brushed with butter (one-quarter of the amount that's normally used in a similar fruit dessert) and honey, the sculptural topping becomes golden and flaky in the oven. (If you prefer, you can brush the phyllo with olive oil instead.) SERVES 6

1½ cups cranberries (fresh or thawed frozen)

1 teaspoon cornstarch

1 teaspoon ground cinnamon

½ teaspoon coarse salt

½ cup honey

3 small or 2 large McIntosh apples (about 1 pound), cored and cut into 1½-inch wedges

2 tablespoons unsalted butter

6 sheets phyllo dough

Preheat oven to 375°F. In an 8-inch square baking dish, toss cranberries with cornstarch, ½ teaspoon cinnamon, and ¼ teaspoon salt. Drizzle with ¼ cup honey. Arrange apples on top of cranberries in one layer, skin sides down. Drizzle with remaining 3 tablespoons honey. Sprinkle with remaining ¼ teaspoon cinnamon and ¼ teaspoon salt.

Melt together butter, remaining 1 tablespoon honey, and remaining ¼ teaspoon cinnamon. Working with one sheet of phyllo at a time, and keeping the others covered with plastic wrap, brush very lightly with butter mixture. Lay a second sheet over first and brush with butter mixture. Repeat with one more sheet. Tear phyllo crosswise into 4 pieces, and loosely crumple (as you would a tissue) as you place on top of apples. Repeat with remaining 3 sheets of phyllo and butter mixture.

Bake for 20 minutes, then reduce oven temperature to 350°F. Bake, rotating dish halfway through, until juices bubble in center and apples are tender, 40 to 50 minutes more. If top darkens too quickly, tent with foil. Cool 30 minutes before serving. (Crunch is best the day it's made.)

Berry Cobbler with Cornmeal Biscuits

Corn and berries are two of summer's signature ingredients. In this ultimate summer cobbler, the airy Cornmeal Drop Biscuits (made with fine whole-grain cornmeal) from page 53 are set over a cinnamon-spiced berry filling before baking. SERVES 8

For the biscuits

- 1½ cups all-purpose flour
- ¾ cup fine yellow cornmeal
- 2 tablespoons natural cane sugar, plus more for sprinkling
- 2 teaspoons baking powder
- ½ teaspoon baking soda
- 1 teaspoon coarse salt
- 1 stick (½ cup) cold unsalted butter, cut into small pieces
- 1 cup milk

  Heavy cream, for brushing

For the filling

- ¼ teaspoon ground cinnamon
- ½ cup natural cane sugar
- 3 tablespoons cornstarch
- 6 cups (3 pints) fresh blackberries or raspberries (or a mix of both)

  Whipped cream or ice cream, for serving (optional)

Make the biscuits: Preheat oven to 375°F. In a large bowl, whisk together flour, cornmeal, 2 tablespoons sugar, baking powder, baking soda, and salt. Using a pastry blender, cut in butter until mixture resembles coarse meal with a few pea-size pieces remaining.

Pour in milk and mix with a fork until dough just comes together. The dough will be slightly sticky (do not overmix).

Make the filling: In another bowl, whisk together cinnamon, sugar, and cornstarch. Add berries and toss gently to coat. Transfer mixture to an 8-inch square or 1½-quart baking dish. Drop 8 mounds of dough over the berries, spacing evenly. Brush dough with heavy cream and sprinkle with sugar.

Bake, rotating dish halfway through, until berries are bubbling in center and biscuits are golden brown, 45 to 50 minutes. Transfer dish to a wire rack and let cool slightly, about 30 minutes. Serve with whipped cream or ice cream, if desired. (Cobbler is best the day it's made.)

Cakes and Cupcakes

Muesli Coffee Cake

Apple-Cider Doughnut Cake

Orange-Barley Pound Cake

Lemon-Cornmeal Cake

Zucchini-Almond Cake

Spelt Layer Cake with Whipped
Cream and Berries

Chocolate Beet Cake

Vegan German Chocolate
Cake

Chocolate Buckwheat Torte

Hummingbird Cake

Oat Roulade with Berry Cream

Flourless Chocolate-Walnut
Torte

Sweet Potato–Cheesecake
Squares

Seeded Saratoga Torte

Coconut-Pistachio Financiers

Lemon-Yogurt Cupcakes

Hazelnut Carrot–Oat
Cupcakes

Gingerbread-Pumpkin
Cakes

Muesli Coffee Cake

A combination of whole-wheat flour and all-purpose flour comes together with sour cream and a layer of fresh blueberries to make a rich, tender coffee cake. Get a subtle crunch on top by sprinkling it with a mix of homemade muesli and honey. You can also use three-quarters of a cup store-bought muesli for the topping. Look for unsweetened brands and toss with honey as directed. MAKES ONE 9½-INCH CAKE

For the topping

- ½ cup old-fashioned rolled oats
- 1½ tablespoons chopped almonds
- 1½ tablespoons dried blueberries or golden raisins
- 1 tablespoon sunflower seeds
- 2 tablespoons honey

For the cake

- 1½ sticks (¾ cup) unsalted butter, room temperature, plus more for pan
- 1½ cups all-purpose flour, plus more for dusting
- 1½ cups whole-wheat flour
- 1½ teaspoons baking powder
- ½ teaspoon baking soda
- ¾ teaspoon coarse salt
- 1¾ cups natural cane sugar
- 4 large eggs, room temperature
- 2 teaspoons vanilla extract
- 1 cup sour cream
- 1 pint fresh blueberries (2 cups)
  Drizzly Glaze (page 287)

Make the topping: In a small bowl, toss together oats, almonds, dried blueberries, and sunflower seeds. Stir in honey.

Make the cake: Preheat oven to 350°F. Butter a 9½-inch tube pan; dust with all-purpose flour. In a bowl, whisk together both flours, baking powder, baking soda, and salt. In another bowl, beat butter with an electric mixer on medium until smooth, about 1 minute. Gradually beat in sugar until mixture is pale and fluffy, about 2 minutes. Add eggs, one at a time, beating to combine after each; then beat in vanilla. Add flour mixture in three batches, alternating with two additions of sour cream, beating until just combined (do not overmix).

Spread half the batter in prepared pan. Top evenly with blueberries. Spread remaining batter on top, then crumble topping over batter, pressing gently to adhere. Bake, rotating pan halfway through, until a tester inserted into center comes out clean, about 1 hour 10 minutes (if cake is browning too quickly, tent with foil). Let cool completely in pan on a wire rack, at least 1 hour 30 minutes, before removing from pan.

Pour Drizzly Glaze over the cooled cake; let set 20 minutes before serving. (Cake can be kept, covered, at room temperature up to 2 days.)

Apple-Cider Doughnut Cake

If you love the apple-cider doughnuts often sold at farmers' markets, you'll love this cake! Baked in a Bundt pan, it's essentially a giant cakey doughnut made a little more wholesome with whole-wheat flour. A blend of olive oil and apple-sauce helps keep it moist. MAKES ONE 10-INCH CAKE

- 2 tablespoons unsalted butter, melted, plus more for pan
- 2 cups all-purpose flour, plus more for pan
- 1 cup whole-wheat flour
- 1½ teaspoons baking powder
- 1½ teaspoons ground cinnamon
- ½ teaspoon baking soda
- ¾ teaspoon coarse salt
- 1¾ cups natural cane sugar
- 1 cup pure apple cider
- ¾ cup extra-virgin olive oil
- ¾ cup unsweetened applesauce
- 2 teaspoons vanilla extract
- 3 large eggs, room temperature

Preheat oven to 350°F. Butter and flour a 12-cup Bundt pan. In a large bowl, whisk together both flours, baking powder, 1 teaspoon cinnamon, the baking soda, and salt.

In another bowl, whisk together 1½ cups sugar, the apple cider, olive oil, applesauce, vanilla, and eggs. Add egg mixture to flour mixture and whisk until combined. Transfer batter to pan.

Bake, rotating pan halfway through, until a tester inserted in center comes out clean, 45 to 50 minutes. Transfer pan to a wire rack set over a rimmed baking sheet; let cool 15 minutes.

Meanwhile, mix the remaining ¼ cup sugar and ½ teaspoon cinnamon. Turn out warm cake onto rack. Brush cake with melted butter. Sprinkle liberally with cinnamon-sugar. Let cool completely before serving. (Cake can be kept, covered, at room temperature up to 2 days.)

Bundt pans need to be generously buttered and floured so cakes don't stick; use a pastry brush to be sure to get into all the crevices.

Orange-Barley Pound Cake

Barley flour makes this pound cake fine-grained and especially tender. Along with the cream cheese, it also adds a subtle tangy flavor that's lovely with the orange. Don't skip creaming the butter and sugar. That's what helps give pound cake its signature crumb. MAKES ONE 9-INCH LOAF

For the cake

- 1½ sticks (¾ cup) unsalted butter, room temperature, plus more for pan
- 1¼ cups all-purpose flour
- ¾ cup barley flour
- 1½ teaspoons baking powder
- ½ teaspoon coarse salt
- 1 navel orange
- 1½ cups natural cane sugar
- 4 ounces cream cheese, room temperature
- 1 teaspoon vanilla extract
- 3 large eggs, room temperature

For the topping

- 1 cup confectioners' sugar
- 2 teaspoons fresh orange juice
- 1 teaspoon orange liqueur, such as Gran Marnier
- Finely grated orange zest, for garnish

Make the cake: Preheat oven to 325°F with rack in lower third. Butter a 9-by-5-inch loaf pan. In a bowl, whisk together both flours, the baking powder, and salt.

Using a peeler, remove zest from half the orange, removing as little white pith as possible. In a food processor, pulse zest with sugar until fine.

In another bowl, with an electric mixer, beat butter and cream cheese on medium until smooth. Add orange sugar and beat on high until pale and fluffy, about 5 minutes. Scrape down sides of bowl. Mix in vanilla.

Add eggs, one at a time, beating after each addition and scraping down sides of bowl as needed. With mixer on low, add flour mixture, mixing until just incorporated. Pour batter into prepared pan; tap on counter and smooth the top.

Bake, rotating pan halfway through, until golden brown and a tester inserted into center comes out clean, about 1 hour and 15 minutes (tent with foil if browning too quickly). Transfer pan to a wire rack and let cake cool, 30 minutes. Remove from pan and let cool completely on rack.

Make the topping: In a bowl, whisk together confectioners' sugar, orange juice, and liqueur until smooth. Spread over pound cake and sprinkle with grated orange zest. (Cake can kept, covered, at room temperature up to 2 days.)

Lemon-Cornmeal Cake

Based on an Italian-style cornmeal torte, this gluten-free cake is enriched and made flavorful with extra-virgin olive oil and ground almonds instead of butter. Pulsing the lemon zest with the sugar and almonds helps distribute its flavor evenly through the cake. Using lemon juice to sour the milk allows it to stand in for buttermilk while further enhancing the lemon flavor. MAKES ONE 9-INCH CAKE

¾ cup extra-virgin olive oil, plus more for pan

½ cup milk

Finely grated zest and juice of 1 lemon

1½ cups raw almonds, finely chopped

1 cup natural cane sugar

1 cup fine yellow cornmeal

1½ teaspoons baking powder

½ teaspoon baking soda

½ teaspoon coarse salt

3 large eggs, room temperature

1 teaspoon almond extract

Confectioners' sugar, for dusting

Preheat oven to 325°F. Oil a 9-inch springform pan. In a bowl, combine milk and lemon juice; let stand until thickened, about 5 minutes.

In a food processor, pulse almonds, cane sugar, and zest until finely ground. Transfer mixture to a large bowl. Stir in cornmeal, baking powder, baking soda, and salt. Add oil, eggs, and almond extract to milk mixture, and whisk until combined. Stir into cornmeal mixture.

Pour batter into prepared pan. Bake, rotating pan halfway through, until cake is golden and a tester inserted into center comes out clean, about 55 minutes. Let cool completely in pan on a wire rack. Unmold and dust with confectioners' sugar just before serving. (Cake can be kept, covered, at room temperature up to 2 days.)

Zucchini-Almond Cake

Almond flour creates the structure for this single-layer gluten-free (and Passover-friendly) cake, while potato starch lightens the texture and zucchini keeps it moist. Cream cheese frosting makes it birthday-worthy.

MAKES ONE 8-INCH CAKE

For the cake

- 4 tablespoons unsalted butter, melted, plus more for pan
- 1½ cups almond flour
- ¼ cup plus 2 tablespoons potato starch
- 1¼ teaspoons baking powder
- ¼ teaspoon fine salt
- 3 large eggs, room temperature
- ½ cup packed light brown sugar
- 1 tablespoon vanilla extract
- 1 cup finely grated zucchini, squeezed of excess liquid (see page 288)

For the frosting

- 5 tablespoons unsalted butter, room temperature
- 1 teaspoon vanilla extract
- 8 ounces cream cheese, room temperature
- ⅓ cup confectioners' sugar

Make the cake: Preheat oven to 350°F. Butter an 8-inch round cake pan. Line bottom with parchment round; butter paper. In a bowl, whisk together almond flour, potato starch, baking powder, and salt.

Set a large heatproof bowl over a pot with 1 inch simmering water. Add eggs and whisk until foamy, about 1 minute. Whisk in brown sugar until mixture is fluffy and sugar is dissolved, 3 minutes. Remove bowl from pot and, with a mixer, whisk on high until mixture is pale, thick, and cool to touch, 7 to 10 minutes.

With a flexible spatula, gently fold in melted butter, flour mixture, vanilla, and zucchini. Pour into pan and bake, rotating pan halfway through, until cake is golden brown and a tester inserted in center comes out with moist crumbs, 25 to 30 minutes. Transfer pan to a wire rack and let cake cool completely. Invert onto a serving platter.

Make the frosting: In a bowl, with an electric mixer, beat together butter, vanilla, and cream cheese on medium-high until fluffy, about 3 minutes. Add confectioners' sugar and beat until combined; spread on top of cake. (Cake can be refrigerated, covered, up to 2 days.)

Spelt Layer Cake with Whipped Cream and Berries

Here is a whole-grain take on a summer birthday cake, complete with lightly sweetened whipped cream and fresh berries for topping. You can use a nice fruit jam in place of the berries sandwiched between the layers, or beneath the whipped cream on top. MAKES ONE 9-INCH DOUBLE-LAYER CAKE

For the cake

- 2 sticks (1 cup) unsalted butter, room temperature, plus more for pans
- 3 cups spelt flour, plus more for pans
- 1 tablespoon baking powder
- 1 teaspoon coarse salt
- 1½ cups natural cane sugar
- 4 large eggs, room temperature
- 2 teaspoons vanilla extract
- 1¼ cups milk

For the topping

- 2 cups heavy cream
- 2 tablespoons raw sugar, such as turbinado
- 1 quart fresh raspberries, blueberries, or strawberries (about 4 cups), hulled and sliced, if large

Make the cake: Preheat oven to 350°F. Butter two 9-inch round cake pans and dust with flour, tapping out excess. In a bowl, whisk together flour, baking powder, and salt.

In another bowl, with an electric mixer, beat butter and sugar on medium until pale and fluffy, 3 to 4 minutes, scraping down the sides of the bowl as needed. Beat in eggs, one at a time, then beat in vanilla. With the mixer on low, add flour mixture in three parts, alternating with milk and beginning and ending with flour; beat just until combined after each addition.

Divide batter evenly between prepared pans and smooth the tops. Bake, rotating pans halfway through, until cakes are golden brown and a cake tester inserted in centers comes out clean, 30 to 35 minutes. Transfer pans to wire racks and let cool, 20 minutes. Invert cakes onto rack and let cool completely.

Make the topping: In a large bowl, with an electric mixer, whisk cream and sugar to soft peaks. Continue whisking until stiff peaks form. Transfer one cake to a serving plate. Spread with 1 cup whipped cream and layer with half the fruit. Top with remaining cake round, and spread with remaining whipped cream, leaving sides of cake bare. Top with remaining fruit and serve. (Cake is best the day it's made.)

5 Easy Cake Finishes

Each of the following recipes relies on an unexpected new pantry ingredient, and yields enough to cover a 9-inch double-layer cake or 24 cupcakes.

1 Salted Chocolate Vegan Ganache

Makes about 2½ cups

Set 10 ounces chopped bittersweet chocolate in a heatproof bowl. In a small saucepan, bring 1¾ cups coconut milk (from one 14-ounce can) just to a boil. Pour milk over chocolate and let stand 2 minutes; then stir with a flexible spatula until ganache is thick and glossy. Add a large pinch of flaky salt. Let cool to room temperature, stirring occasionally, until thick and spreadable. Alternatively, you can use it as a glaze while still warm; drizzle over cakes or dip top of cupcakes in it. Ganache can be refrigerated up to 2 days. Bring to room temperature and stir before using.

2 Fruit Glaze

Makes 1¼ cups

In a blender, puree 1 cup fresh or thawed frozen raspberries or pitted sweet cherries until smooth. Strain into a bowl through a fine-mesh sieve. In another bowl, whisk together 3 cups sifted confectioners' sugar with ½ cup strained fruit puree. Dip cupcakes into glaze, or pour glaze over single cake layers. Let glaze set 15 minutes before serving.

3 Honey Whipped Yogurt

Makes about 3 cups

This is great as a dollop alongside chocolate cakes or those made with fruit. In a bowl, whisk together 3 cups Greek yogurt, 3 tablespoons honey, and ½ teaspoon vanilla extract. Whipped yogurt can be refrigerated for up to 5 days.

4 Vegan Maple Cream Frosting

Makes about 3 cups

With an electric mixer, beat 1½ cups maple butter (available at specialty food shops) until light and smooth, 1 minute. Add ¾ cup melted coconut oil, 1 tablespoon at a time, fully incorporating the oil before adding more. If the coconut oil is not incorporating, transfer bowl to freezer for 1 to 2 minutes to let mixture set. When oil is fully incorporated, frosting should be light in color and fluffy in texture. Use immediately.

5 Goat Cheese Frosting

Makes about 3 cups

Try this in place of cream cheese frosting on carrot, red velvet, and spice cakes. With an electric mixer, beat 8 ounces room-temperature goat cheese with 1 pound room-temperature cream cheese until smooth and combined. Gradually add ½ cup confectioners' sugar, and beat until smooth and creamy. Frosting can be refrigerated up to 3 days. Bring to room temperature and stir before using.

Chocolate Beet Cake

You won't taste the pureed beets, but they make this cake extra moist and fudgy, even with the addition of whole-grain spelt flour. The beets also play up the cake's full-bodied, not-too-sweet flavor. MAKES ONE 9-INCH CAKE

---

4 medium (1½ pounds) beets, trimmed, peeled, and cut into 2-inch chunks

¼ cup safflower oil, plus more for pan

1 cup spelt flour

1 cup all-purpose flour

1½ cups natural cane sugar

½ cup unsweetened Dutch-process cocoa powder

1½ teaspoons baking soda

¾ teaspoon coarse salt

2 large eggs, room temperature

¾ cup warm water

1 teaspoon vanilla extract

Chocolate Ganache Frosting (page 287)

Place beets in a steamer basket set in a saucepan filled with 2 inches of simmering water. Cover and steam until beets are tender when pierced with a sharp knife, about 25 minutes. Let cool slightly, then puree in a food processor until smooth.

Preheat oven to 350°F. Oil one 9-inch square or round cake pan. Line bottom with a parchment and oil parchment. In a large bowl, whisk together both flours, sugar, cocoa powder, baking soda, and salt. Whisk in eggs, water, oil, vanilla, and 1¼ cups beet puree (reserve remaining puree for another use).

Pour batter into prepared pan. Bake, rotating pan halfway through, until cake is set and a cake tester inserted in center comes out clean, about 35 minutes. Transfer pan to a wire rack and let cake cool, 20 minutes. Invert cake onto rack and let cool completely.

Place cake on a cake plate and spread evenly with chocolate ganache. (Cake can be kept, covered, up to 2 days.)

Vegan German Chocolate Cake

Despite its name, this cake is actually not German at all: It was created in the United States and named to showcase German's brand sweet chocolate. This version has a few notable updates. It relies on cocoa powder instead of melted chocolate for flavors. It also tastes extra-coconutty (and happens to be vegan) because both the cake and filling contain coconut milk and oil. To keep the sweetness in check, it is topped with a bittersweet chocolate ganache instead of more filling. MAKES ONE 9-INCH TRIPLE-LAYER CAKE

For the cake

- 1 cup melted virgin coconut oil, plus more for pans
- ⅔ cup unsweetened Dutch-process cocoa powder, plus more for dusting
- 3 cups all-purpose flour
- 2 cups natural cane sugar
- 2 teaspoons baking soda
- 1 teaspoon coarse salt
- 2 tablespoons instant espresso powder
- 2 cups unsweetened coconut milk
- 2 teaspoons vanilla extract
- ¼ cup apple cider vinegar

If you're using canned coconut milk, make sure it's full fat and doesn't contain any additives.

Make the cake: Preheat oven to 350°F. Oil three 8-inch round cake pans and line with parchment rounds; oil parchment and dust with cocoa powder.

In a large bowl, whisk together flour, sugar, cocoa, baking soda, and salt. In another bowl, whisk together coconut oil, espresso powder, coconut milk, and vanilla. Whisk milk mixture into flour mixture until combined. Quickly stir in vinegar until incorporated.

Divide batter evenly among prepared pans. Bake, rotating pans halfway through, until tops spring back when lightly touched, 30 to 32 minutes. Transfer pans to wire racks and let cakes cool, 10 minutes. Invert cakes onto wire racks and let cool completely.

For the filling

- 2 cups unsweetened shredded coconut
- 1½ cups natural cane sugar
- ¼ cup plus 2 tablespoons water
- 2 teaspoons melted virgin coconut oil
- 1½ cups chopped pecans, toasted (see page 288)
- 1 cup unsweetened coconut milk
- ½ teaspoon coarse salt
- ½ teaspoon vanilla extract

For the ganache frosting

- 4 ounces bittersweet chocolate, finely chopped
- ½ cup unsweetened coconut milk

Make the filling: Set coconut in a large bowl. In a small, heavy-bottomed saucepan, combine ½ cup sugar and ¼ cup water. Cook, stirring occasionally, until mixture just comes to a boil and becomes clear. Pour over unsweetened coconut, add coconut oil, and stir together until combined. Let cool for about 5 minutes, then add pecans and toss.

In same small saucepan, combine remaining 1 cup sugar with remaining 2 tablespoons water. Place over high heat; cook, brushing down sides of pan with a wet pastry brush, until caramel is amber, 6 to 8 minutes. Immediately remove from heat, and gradually add coconut milk. (Be careful, as it will splatter.) Return caramel to medium heat, and cook until slightly thickened, 3 to 4 minutes. Add salt and vanilla; stir warm caramel into shredded coconut mixture. Let cool to room temperature.

Make the ganache frosting: Put chocolate in a large bowl. In a small saucepan, bring coconut milk just to a boil. Pour coconut milk over chocolate, and let stand 3 minutes; stir until smooth. Let stand until thick and spreadable, stirring occasionally, about 1 hour.

Place one cake on a cake plate or platter, flat side down; spread half the coconut filling evenly across the top. Place a second cake, flat side up, on top of first layer; spread with remaining filling. Place remaining cake, flat side up, on top; spread top evenly with ganache, leaving the cake sides exposed. Refrigerate for 30 minutes before slicing. (The cake can be kept, covered, at room temperature for up to 1 day. Unfilled cake layers can be tightly wrapped and kept at room temperature overnight.)

Chocolate Buckwheat Torte

This gluten-free cake has a lighter texture than the classic flourless chocolate cake, thanks to the addition of buckwheat flour and ground almonds. Buckwheat flour complements the grown-up, earthier side of chocolate. We like the torte with chai-flavored or vanilla ice cream. MAKES ONE 9-INCH TORTE

1 stick (½ cup) unsalted butter, cut into pieces, plus more for pan

6 ounces semisweet chocolate, coarsely chopped

¼ cup blanched almonds, toasted (see page 288)

⅓ cup buckwheat flour

¼ teaspoon coarse salt

¼ teaspoon ground cinnamon

4 large eggs, room temperature

½ cup packed light brown sugar

Confectioners' sugar, for dusting

Ice cream, for serving (optional)

Preheat oven to 350°F. Butter a 9-inch springform pan. Line with a parchment round; butter parchment.

In a heatproof bowl set over a pan of simmering water, melt together butter and chocolate. Let cool.

In a food processor, pulse almonds until finely ground. Add flour, salt, and cinnamon, and pulse until combined.

With an electric mixer, whisk eggs and brown sugar on high until pale and thick, about 6 minutes. Fold in chocolate mixture, then flour mixture.

Pour into prepared pan. Bake, rotating pan halfway through, until cake is puffed and a tester inserted in center comes out clean, about 25 minutes. Transfer pan to a wire rack and let cake cool, 10 minutes; then release sides of pan and remove. Let cake cool completely.

Dust with confectioners' sugar before serving. Serve with ice cream, if desired. (Torte can be kept at room temperature, covered, up to 1 day.)

Hummingbird Cake

This classic southern cake—so named because it's supposed to make you hum with delight—can be cloyingly sweet. Enter coconut sugar, a sweetener from the sap of a coconut tree's flower buds. While it has no coconut flavor, it does bring a caramelized, almost savory complexity to baked goods. It's perfect in a cake that's plenty sweet (as well as moist), thanks to the additions of banana and pineapple. MAKES ONE 8-INCH TRIPLE-LAYER CAKE

For the cakes

- ¾ cup safflower oil, plus more for pans
- 3 cups all-purpose flour
- 2 cups coconut sugar
- 2 teaspoons baking powder
- 1 teaspoon ground cinnamon
- ¾ teaspoon baking soda
- ¾ teaspoon coarse salt
- 3 large eggs, room temperature
- 1¾ cups mashed ripe bananas (from about 5 medium)
- 2 teaspoons vanilla extract
- 1 cup chopped fresh pineapple
- 1 cup pecans, finely chopped
- 1 cup unsweetened shredded coconut

  Cream Cheese Frosting, page 287

  Large unsweetened coconut flakes, toasted, for garnish (see page 288)

Make the cakes: Preheat oven to 350°F. Oil three 8-inch round cake pans. Line bottoms with parchment rounds; oil parchment.

In a bowl, whisk together flour, coconut sugar, baking powder, cinnamon, baking soda, and salt. In another bowl, whisk eggs, oil, bananas, and vanilla. Stir banana mixture into flour mixture until just combined (do not overmix). Fold in pineapple, pecans, and coconut (the batter will be thick).

Divide batter evenly among pans and smooth the tops. Bake, rotating pans halfway through, until a tester inserted in centers comes out clean, 20 to 25 minutes. Transfer pans to wire racks and let cakes cool, 20 minutes. Invert cakes onto racks and let cool completely.

Place one cake on a cake platter, flat side down. Spread about ¾ cup frosting evenly across top. Place a second cake, flat side up, on top of first layer. Spread with another ¾ cup frosting. Place remaining cake, flat side up, on top; spread remaining frosting evenly across top and sides of cake. Garnish with coconut flakes. Refrigerate for 30 minutes before serving. (Cake can be refrigerated, covered, up to 2 days; bring to a cool room temperature before serving.)

Oat Roulade with Berry Cream

This old-fashioned jelly roll is made with ground oats acting as the flour. The oat flour here is left unsifted, creating a cake with a pleasingly rustic texture that's perfect with a silky, jam-sweetened whipped cream. It's delicious with a glass of dessert wine, such as vin santo or sauternes. MAKES ONE 11-INCH CAKE

---

4 tablespoons unsalted butter, melted, plus more for pan

1 cup old-fashioned rolled oats

4 large eggs, separated, yolks lightly beaten

½ cup natural cane sugar

Pinch coarse salt

Confectioners' sugar, for dusting

1 cup heavy cream

¼ cup jam, such as blackberry

Preheat oven to 350°F. Butter a rimmed 11-by-17-inch baking sheet, and line with parchment; butter parchment. In a food processor, grind oats to a fine meal. Dust pan with ¼ cup ground oats, tapping out excess.

In a bowl, with an electric mixer, whisk egg whites with ¼ cup cane sugar on medium speed until stiff peaks form, about 3 minutes. Combine yolks with remaining ¼ cup cane sugar in a clean bowl and whisk on high, 3 minutes, until tripled in volume.

Carefully fold yolks into egg whites, followed by the remaining ¾ cup ground oats and the salt. Drizzle melted butter around edge of bowl; carefully fold in just until combined (do not overmix.)

Transfer batter to prepared pan and spread to edges with an offset spatula. Bake, rotating pan halfway through, until cake is lightly golden and springs back to touch, 15 minutes. Run a knife around sides of cake to loosen. Invert onto a kitchen towel dusted with confectioners' sugar (see next page for how-to); remove parchment. Roll cake in towel, starting at a short end. Let cool, seam side down.

Whisk cream to soft peaks. Fold in jam. Unroll cake and spread with berry cream, leaving a ½-inch border. Reroll cake without towel, starting at the same short side. Refrigerate at least 30 minutes and up to 3 hours. Serve dusted with confectioners' sugar.

How to Form a Roulade

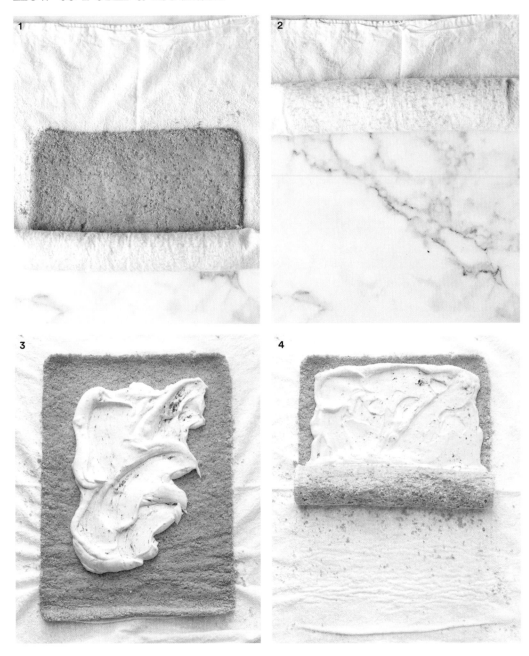

1 Invert just-baked cake onto a kitchen towel dusted with confectioners' sugar. Roll cake in towel, starting at a short end. **2** Let cake cool completely seam side down. **3** Unroll cake and spread with whipped-cream mixture, leaving ½-inch border. **4** Reroll cake without towel, starting from the same short side.

Once the cake is rolled with filling, refrigerate until set, at least 30 minutes and up to 3 hours. Finish with a generous dusting of confectioners' sugar.

Flourless Chocolate-Walnut Torte

Luscious flourless chocolate cake is a staple dessert for people who follow a gluten-free diet. Many of these cakes rely on butter for richness, but the secret to this dairy-free recipe is coconut oil. If you serve the cake chilled, it tastes even fudgier. MAKES ONE 8-INCH TORTE

- ½ cup plus 1 teaspoon virgin coconut oil, plus more for pan
- ¼ cup unsweetened Dutch-process cocoa powder, plus more for pan
- ½ cup walnuts, toasted (see page 288); plus 2 tablespoons, toasted and finely chopped walnuts, for garnish
- 10 ounces bittersweet chocolate, finely chopped (1⅔ cups)
- 1¼ cups natural cane sugar
- 4 large eggs, room temperature
- 1 teaspoon vanilla extract
- ½ teaspoon coarse salt

Preheat oven to 350°F. Oil an 8-inch round cake pan. Line bottom with a parchment round; oil parchment and dust with cocoa. In a food processor, pulse ½ cup walnuts until finely ground.

In a heatproof bowl set over a pan of simmering water, melt together ½ cup oil and 8 ounces (1⅓ cups) chocolate, stirring, until smooth. Remove from heat and whisk in sugar until combined. Whisk in eggs, one at a time. Whisk in cocoa, vanilla, and salt. Fold in ground walnuts.

Spread batter in prepared pan. Bake, rotating pan halfway through, until cake is set, about 35 minutes. Transfer pan to a wire rack and let cake cool completely, preferably overnight. Run a knife around edge to loosen; remove from pan. Transfer cake to a serving plate.

In a heatproof bowl set over a pan of simmering water, melt remaining 2 ounces (⅓ cup) chocolate and remaining 1 teaspoon oil, stirring, until smooth. Pour over center of cake and spread to cover top. Sprinkle chopped walnuts in center. Cut into wedges and serve. (Torte can be refrigerated, covered, up to 1 day.)

Sweet Potato-Cheesecake Squares

Try these cheesecake squares in place of pumpkin pie for Thanksgiving or at any autumn gathering. Thanks to the ricotta and Greek yogurt, the filling has a lovely silky texture. It wouldn't be cheesecake without a buttery press-in cookie crust. If you are so inclined, bake the graham crackers yourself using the recipe on page 124. MAKES ONE 9-BY-13-INCH CAKE

---

2 medium sweet potatoes
(1½ pounds total)

18 graham crackers
(9 ounces total)

1 cup natural cane sugar

1 stick (½ cup) plus
3 tablespoons unsalted
butter, melted

½ teaspoon fine salt

1½ cups fresh ricotta

½ cup plain Greek yogurt

4 large eggs, room
temperature

Lightly sweetened whipped
cream, for serving (optional)

Preheat oven to 375°F. Bake sweet potatoes until tender, about 1 hour. Remove from oven and let cool slightly, then discard skins and mash flesh with a fork (you should have 1½ cups).

In a food processor, pulse graham crackers until finely ground (you should have about 2¼ cups). Add ⅓ cup sugar, 1 stick melted butter, and ¼ teaspoon salt, and pulse until combined. Firmly press mixture into bottom of a 9-by-13-inch baking dish. Bake until crust is dry and set, about 12 minutes. Remove from oven and reduce temperature to 325°F.

Meanwhile, in clean bowl of food processor, puree sweet potatoes, ricotta, yogurt, eggs, remaining ¼ teaspoon salt, remaining 3 table-spoons butter, and remaining ⅔ cup sugar.

Pour into crust and bake, rotating pan halfway through, until just set in center, 30 to 35 minutes. Let cool on a wire rack, 30 minutes. Refrigerate until cold, at least 1 hour or overnight. Cut into squares and top with whipped cream, if desired. (Cake can be refrigerated, covered, up to 1 day.)

Bake and mash the potatoes up to three days ahead. Store in an airtight container in the refrigerator.

Seeded Saratoga Torte

Crushed graham crackers are folded into a pavlova-like meringue in this Australian classic. This version boasts a hefty dose of seeds—including ground toasted sunflower, pumpkin, and sesame, as well as whole poppy seeds—in the torte itself and sprinkled over the whipped cream on top. SERVES 8 TO 10

- 2 tablespoons sesame seeds
- ¼ cup hulled pumpkin seeds (pepitas)
- ¼ cup sunflower seeds
- 2 tablespoons poppy seeds
- 3 large egg whites, room temperature
- ¾ cup plus 1 tablespoon superfine sugar
- 1 teaspoon vanilla extract
- ⅛ teaspoon coarse salt
- 1 sleeve (5 ounces) graham crackers, finely ground with some bigger pieces remaining (1¼ cups)
- ½ cup cherry or other red-fruit preserves
- ¾ cup heavy cream

Superfine sugar dissolves best in a meringue. If you can't find it, you can pulse granulated sugar a few times in a food processor; re-measure and add more sugar, if necessary, before using.

Preheat oven to 350°F. Line a rimmed baking sheet with parchment. Trace an 8-inch circle on top with a pencil; turn marked side down.

Spread sesame, pumpkin, and sunflower seeds in a single layer on another rimmed baking sheet. Toast, stirring once, until golden, about 12 minutes. Let cool completely. Finely grind baked seeds in a spice grinder or food processor; transfer to a bowl. Stir in poppy seeds.

In a large bowl, with an electric mixer, whisk egg whites on medium-high until soft peaks form. Slowly add ¾ cup sugar, whisking until stiff, glossy peaks form. Whisk in vanilla and salt. Fold in graham-cracker crumbs and ¾ cup seed mixture. Dab meringue under corners of parchment to secure to baking sheet. Using an offset spatula, spread meringue within marked circle. Bake, rotating sheet halfway through, until top is crisp and brown, about 25 minutes. Transfer sheet to wire rack and let torte cool completely.

Spread preserves on top of meringue. In another bowl, whisk cream with remaining 1 tablespoon sugar until soft peaks form. Dollop on top of preserves, and sprinkle with remaining seed mixture. Cut into wedges with a sharp knife, wiping between slices, and serve. (Torte is best the day it's made.)

Coconut-Pistachio Financiers

Financiers are pleasantly dense, brown-buttery little French cakes that were named because the originals resembled bankers' bars of gold. With ground pistachios (in place of the usual almonds), coconut (flour and shredded flakes) and cardamom in the batter, these exotic financiers have Indian flavors. (They're also gluten-free.) They're perfect teatime or on-the-go snacks. MAKES 18

¾ cup shelled unsalted pistachios

1 stick (½ cup) unsalted butter

5 cardamom pods, crushed

1 vanilla bean, split lengthwise and scraped

⅓ cup coconut flour

¼ cup unsweetened shredded coconut

½ cup natural cane sugar

½ teaspoon coarse salt

4 large egg whites, lightly beaten until foamy

Preheat oven to 350°F. Line a mini-muffin tin with 18 paper liners. Using a coffee or spice grinder, grind ½ cup pistachios into a fine powder. Finely chop remaining ¼ cup.

In a small saucepan, melt butter over medium heat. Remove from heat, and add cardamom pods and vanilla bean and seeds; cover and let stand for 10 minutes. Strain butter, discarding solids.

In a large bowl, whisk together the finely ground pistachios, the coconut flour, shredded coconut, sugar, and salt. With an electric mixer, beat in egg whites on medium until incorporated; quickly fold in melted butter.

Divide batter evenly among prepared muffin cups (about 1½ tablespoons per cup). Sprinkle tops with chopped pistachios. Bake, rotating pan halfway through, until a cake tester inserted into centers comes out clean, 12 to 14 minutes. Transfer pan to wire rack and let financiers cool completely. (Cakes can be kept in an airtight container at room temperature up to 3 days.)

Lemon-Yogurt Cupcakes

White whole-wheat flour makes these cupcakes more wholesome than most, without compromising their delicate lemony flavor. Made with less butter and sugar than usual, the cakes take a cue from a classic French cake that uses yogurt to keep it moist. Raspberries color and flavor the frosting naturally. MAKES 1 DOZEN

For the cupcakes

- 1¾ cups white whole-wheat flour
- 1¼ teaspoons baking powder
- ¼ teaspoon baking soda
- ½ teaspoon coarse salt
- 4 tablespoons unsalted butter, room temperature
- ¾ cup natural cane sugar
- 1 teaspoon finely grated lemon zest, plus 2 teaspoons fresh lemon juice
- 1 teaspoon vanilla extract
- 1 large egg, room temperature
- 1½ cups plain yogurt

For the frosting

- ¾ cup fresh raspberries
- 1 tablespoon natural cane sugar
- 1½ sticks (¾ cup) unsalted butter, room temperature
- 2 cups confectioners' sugar, sifted

Make the cupcakes: Preheat oven to 350°F. Line 12 muffin cups with paper liners. In a bowl, whisk together flour, baking powder, baking soda, and salt. In another bowl, with an electric mixer, beat butter, sugar, and lemon zest on medium until well combined, about 3 minutes. Beat in lemon juice, vanilla, and egg. Add flour mixture in three batches, alternating with two additions of yogurt and beating until just combined (do not overmix).

Divide batter evenly among muffin cups. Bake, rotating pan halfway through, until cakes are golden and a tester inserted in centers comes out clean, 18 to 20 minutes. Transfer tin to a wire rack and let cakes cool completely.

Make the frosting: In a food processor, puree berries with cane sugar until smooth. Pass mixture through a fine sieve into a bowl, pressing to extract as much liquid as possible.

In another bowl, with an electric mixer, beat butter on medium-high until pale and fluffy, 2 minutes. With mixer on medium, add confectioners' sugar, ½ cup at a time, beating well after each addition. Beat in berry puree.

Use an offset spatula to spread frosting over each cupcake. Unfrosted cupcakes can be kept in an airtight container at room temperature up to 2 days. Frosting can be refrigerated up to 2 days; bring to room temperature, and beat on low until smooth again before using.

Hazelnut Carrot-Oat Cupcakes

With oat flour and ground hazelnuts, these carrot cupcakes are a twist on the classic carrot cake. Cream cheese frosting is the signature accompaniment, but try the goat cheese frosting on page 195, too. MAKES 1 DOZEN

For the cupcakes

- ¾ cup oat flour
- ¾ cup all-purpose flour
- ¾ teaspoon baking soda
- ¼ teaspoon coarse salt
- ¼ cup toasted skinned (see page 288) hazelnuts, finely chopped
- ⅓ cup safflower oil
- ⅓ cup buttermilk
- 2 large eggs, room temperature
- 1 cup natural cane sugar
- 1 teaspoon vanilla extract
- 1 teaspoon finely grated orange zest
- 1 cup packed finely grated peeled carrots (from 3 carrots)

For the frosting

- 8 ounces cream cheese, room temperature
- ½ cup confectioners' sugar
- Pinch coarse salt
- 3 tablespoons hazelnuts, toasted, skinned, and coarsely chopped (see page 288)

Make the cupcakes: Preheat oven to 350°F. Line 12 cups of a muffin tin with paper liners. In a bowl, whisk together both flours, baking soda, salt, and hazelnuts. In another bowl, whisk together oil, buttermilk, eggs, sugar, vanilla, orange zest, and carrots until combined. Fold oil mixture into flour mixture until just combined. Divide batter evenly among muffin cups.

Bake, rotating pan halfway through, until cakes are golden and a toothpick inserted in centers comes out clean, about 23 minutes. Let cupcakes cool in pan 15 minutes, then transfer to a wire rack and let cool completely.

Make the frosting: In a small bowl, stir together cream cheese and confectioners' sugar until smooth; season with salt. Use an offset spatula to spread frosting over each cupcake, then sprinkle with coarsely chopped hazelnuts. (Cupcakes are best the day they're made.)

Gingerbread-Pumpkin Cakes

Canned pumpkin puree makes these molasses-sweetened spice cakes extra moist. Whole-wheat flour adds a distinctively nutty flavor that's delicious with the spices here. The glazed cakes can be baked in French canelé molds, available at baking-supply stores, or muffin tins. If you want to use a 5-by-9-inch loaf pan, bake for 70 minutes. MAKES 18

4 tablespoons unsalted butter, room temperature, plus more for pans

1⅓ cups all-purpose flour, plus more for pans

1 cup whole-wheat flour

2 teaspoons baking powder

1 teaspoon baking soda

1 teaspoon ground ginger

½ teaspoon ground allspice

½ teaspoon ground cinnamon

¼ teaspoon ground cloves

½ teaspoon fine salt

¾ cup natural cane sugar

1 cup canned unsweetened pumpkin puree

½ cup unsulfured molasses

2 large eggs, lightly beaten

½ cup buttermilk

1 cup confectioners' sugar, sifted

2 tablespoons water

Preheat oven to 350°F. Butter and flour 18 canelé molds or muffin cups. In a large bowl, whisk together both flours, baking powder, baking soda, ginger, allspice, cinnamon, cloves, and salt. In another bowl, with an electric mixer, beat butter and cane sugar on medium-high until pale and fluffy, about 3 minutes. Beat in pumpkin puree until smooth, then beat in molasses, eggs, and buttermilk. Add pumpkin mixture to flour mixture in three additions, beating well between each, until combined.

Divide batter among molds and set them on baking sheets. Bake, rotating sheets halfway through, until the cakes are puffed and set, 35 minutes. Transfer molds to wire racks and let cakes cool completely. Remove cakes from molds and set on a rack over a sheet of foil.

In a small bowl, whisk together confectioners' sugar and water. Spoon over cakes and let glaze set, about 15 minutes, before serving. (Cakes can be refrigerated in an airtight container up to 3 days.)

Breads and Rolls

Seeded Savory Quickbread

Whole-Wheat Date Nut Bread

Irish-Style Brown Bread

Soda Bread with Currants and Caraway

Whole-Grain Cornbread

Coconut Banana Bread

Zucchini and Chocolate Loaves

Whole-Grain Pumpkin Bread

Molasses-Oat Bread

Honey Whole-Wheat Bread

No-Knead Seeded Bread

Gluten-Free Sandwich Bread

Whole-Wheat Stollen

Hazelnut Hot-Cross Buns

Honey-Wheat Parker House Rolls

Stuffed Whole-Wheat Flatbreads

Whole-Wheat Pita Bread

Spelt Tortillas

Whole-Wheat Popovers

Seeded English Muffins

Whole-Grain Seeded Wafer Crackers

Rye Soft Pretzels

Whole-Wheat Monkey Bread

Coconut-Pumpkin Bread Pudding

Seeded Savory Quickbread

This robust loaf—chockablock with caraway, flax, sunflower, and black sesame seeds, as well as whole-wheat and spelt flours—comes together in a snap. Spread it with butter and jam for a simple and delicious breakfast, snack on it toasted and topped with ricotta, or layer on sliced hard cheese and avocado for an open-faced sandwich. MAKES ONE 9-INCH LOAF

2 tablespoons extra-virgin olive oil, plus more for pan

2 cups whole-wheat pastry flour

2 cups spelt flour

½ cup plus 2 teaspoons sunflower seeds, toasted (see page 288)

½ cup plus 1 teaspoon black sesame seeds

2 tablespoons plus 1 teaspoon caraway seeds

2 tablespoons plus 1 teaspoon flaxseeds

2 teaspoons baking powder

1 teaspoon baking soda

2 teaspoons coarse salt

1½ cups milk, room temperature

¾ cup buttermilk, room temperature

2 tablespoons honey

Preheat oven to 350°F. Lightly coat a 9-by-5-inch loaf pan with oil. Line with parchment, leaving a 1-inch overhang on long sides. Oil parchment.

In a bowl, whisk together both flours, ½ cup each sunflower and black sesame seeds, 2 tablespoons each caraway and flaxseeds, the baking powder, baking soda, and salt.

In another bowl, stir together milk, buttermilk, honey, and olive oil until honey is dissolved. Add flour mixture; beat with a wooden spoon until combined, about 1 minute. Transfer to prepared pan; sprinkle with remaining seeds, pressing gently to adhere.

Bake, rotating pan halfway through, until a tester inserted in center of the loaf comes out clean, about 65 minutes. Let cool in pan on a wire rack 20 minutes, then turn out bread and let cool completely. (Bread can be tightly wrapped and kept at room temperature up to 3 days or frozen up to 1 month.)

Whole-wheat pastry flour has less protein than regular whole-wheat flour, resulting in a lighter, more tender bread. You can substitute regular whole-wheat flour, but the bread will be slightly more coarse and dense.

Whole-Wheat Date Nut Bread

This date-sweetened whole-wheat quickbread makes a much-appreciated holiday or hostess gift because it holds up well for several days and is a wholesome breakfast treat. A schmear of tangy cream cheese balances the sweet-nutty flavor of the dates and pecans. MAKES ONE 9-INCH LOAF

2 tablespoons safflower oil, plus more for pan

1½ cups hot water

1 cup pitted dates, chopped

1 large egg

1 teaspoon vanilla extract

1 cup all-purpose flour

1 cup whole-wheat flour

1 teaspoon baking soda

¾ teaspoon coarse salt

1 cup pecans, toasted and chopped (see page 288)

¾ cup packed light brown sugar

Preheat oven to 350°F. Lightly coat a 9-by-5-inch loaf pan with oil. In a bowl, pour hot water over dates and let stand until slightly softened, about 5 minutes. Whisk in oil, egg, and vanilla. In another bowl, stir together both flours, baking soda, salt, pecans, and brown sugar. Fold egg mixture into flour mixture until just combined. Pour batter into prepared pan and smooth top.

Bake, rotating pan halfway through, until a tester inserted in center of loaf comes out clean, about 65 minutes. Let cool in pan on a wire rack, 20 minutes, then turn out bread and let cool completely. (Loaf can be tightly wrapped and kept at room temperature up to 3 days.)

Irish-Style Brown Bread

This humble loaf, which gets a small update with the addition of rye flour, is similar to the one you would find every day on the traditional Irish table, served with butter and jam, smoked salmon, or stew. In this version, the dough is cut into six wedges that are baked close together so they form a loaf that's easy to pull apart. If you prefer to make the loaf easier to slice, don't cut through the dough; just use a sharp knife to make shallow slashes before baking. MAKES ONE 6-INCH LOAF

2½ cups whole-wheat flour

1½ cups rye flour

1¼ teaspoons baking soda

1½ teaspoons coarse salt

2 cups buttermilk

Preheat oven to 425°F. In a bowl, whisk together both flours, baking soda, and salt.

Pour buttermilk into flour mixture and stir until just combined; then knead in bowl two or three times until all the flour has been incorporated and a shaggy dough forms.

Form dough into a 6-inch disk. Transfer dough to a parchment-lined sheet. With a sharp knife or bench scraper, cut into 6 wedges, leaving the wedges in place.

Bake, rotating sheet halfway through, until bread is firm and sounds hollow when tapped on the bottom, about 35 minutes. Let cool on sheet on a wire rack. Serve warm or at room temperature. (Bread is best the day it's made.)

Soda Bread with Currants and Caraway

With caraway seeds, currants, butter, egg, and a touch of sugar, this cake-like version of Irish soda is a bit fancy; real Irish soda bread is quite plain. A blend of white whole-wheat flour and oat flour creates a tender, melt-in-the-mouth texture. MAKES ONE 8-INCH LOAF

2 cups white whole-wheat flour

2 cups old-fashioned rolled oats, finely ground

¼ cup natural cane sugar

¾ cup dried currants

1 tablespoon caraway seeds

1 teaspoon baking soda

1 teaspoon coarse salt

6 tablespoons cold unsalted butter, cut into small pieces

1½ cups buttermilk

1 large egg

Preheat oven to 350°F. In a large bowl, whisk together flour, ground oats, sugar, currants, caraway seeds, baking soda, and salt. Add butter and work in with your fingers or a pastry blender until pieces are about the size of small peas. In a separate bowl, whisk together buttermilk and egg. Pour wet ingredients into dry ingredients and stir together just until a soft dough forms.

Transfer dough to a parchment-lined baking sheet. Shape into a round about 6½ inches across and 2 inches high, using lightly moistened fingers. Score an "X" on top of loaf, using a sharp knife or bench scraper.

Bake, rotating sheet halfway through, until the loaf sounds hollow when tapped on the bottom, about 40 minutes. Let cool on sheet on a wire rack 20 minutes, then transfer bread to rack and let cool completely. (Bread can be tightly wrapped and kept at room temperature up to 2 days.)

Whole-Grain Cornbread

With olive oil standing in for the usual butter and whole-wheat flour for white flour, this cornbread is a heartier version, but still richly flavorful. Preheating the pan ensures the bread's edges get nice and crisp.

MAKES ONE 8-INCH LOAF

1 cup medium-grind cornmeal

1 cup whole-wheat flour

¼ cup natural cane sugar

½ teaspoon baking soda

1 tablespoon baking powder

1 teaspoon coarse salt

1 large egg

1 cup buttermilk

¼ cup plus 1 tablespoon extra-virgin olive oil

2 tablespoons honey

Preheat oven to 400°F. Place an 8-inch metal pie dish or cast-iron pan in oven while you prepare batter. In a bowl, whisk together cornmeal, flour, sugar, baking soda, baking powder, and salt. In a small bowl, whisk together egg, buttermilk, and ¼ cup oil. Fold egg mixture into flour mixture and mix until just combined.

Add remaining tablespoon oil to preheated pan, swirling to coat the bottom. Pour in batter and smooth the top.

Bake, rotating pan halfway through, until bread is golden brown and a tester inserted in center of loaf comes out clean, 23 to 25 minutes. Brush with honey, then let cool in pan on a wire rack 20 minutes. Cut into squares or wedges and serve. (Cornbread can be tightly wrapped and kept at room temperature up to 1 day.)

Coconut Banana Bread

Thanks to the addition of coconut in two forms (oil and flour), this banana bread also tastes richly tropical. Bonus: Coconut flour, which has 5 grams of fiber per tablespoon, turns each slice into a higher-fiber treat. MAKES ONE 9-INCH LOAF

½ cup melted virgin coconut oil, plus more for pan

¾ cup all-purpose flour, plus more for pan

½ cup coconut flour

¾ teaspoon baking soda

½ teaspoon coarse salt

1 cup packed dark brown sugar

½ cup buttermilk, room temperature

2 large eggs, room temperature

1 cup mashed ripe bananas (from 2 or 3 medium)

1 teaspoon vanilla extract

¾ cup chopped pecans

Preheat oven to 350°F. Oil and flour a 9-by-5-inch loaf pan. In a bowl, whisk together both flours, baking soda, and salt.

In a large bowl, whisk together oil, brown sugar, buttermilk, eggs, bananas, and vanilla. Fold in flour mixture and pecans. Pour batter into pan.

Bake, rotating pan halfway through, until a tester inserted in center of the loaf comes out clean, 50 to 60 minutes. (Tent with foil if browning too quickly.)

Let cool in pan on a wire rack 20 minutes, then turn out bread and let cool completely. (Banana bread can be tightly wrapped and kept at room temperature up to 3 days.)

Zucchini and Chocolate Loaves

Here is a new (and more wholesome) way to make zucchini bread when the vegetable is in abundance from summer to fall. Whole-grain spelt flour contributes a hearty flavor, and applesauce makes the loaves moister without adding fat. And chunks of bittersweet chocolate throughout take the whole thing over the top. MAKES 4 MINI LOAVES

½ cup safflower oil, plus more for pans

1 cup spelt flour

1 cup all-purpose flour

2¾ teaspoons baking powder

1 teaspoon coarse salt

¾ teaspoon ground cinnamon

3 large eggs, room temperature

½ cup unsweetened applesauce

1¼ cups natural cane sugar

3 cups grated zucchini (see page 288)

2 teaspoons vanilla extract

4 ounces bittersweet chocolate, finely chopped (about ¾ cup)

Preheat oven to 350°F. Oil four 3-by-5½-inch loaf pans. Line each with parchment, leaving 1 inch of overhang on long sides. Oil parchment.

In a bowl, whisk together both flours, baking powder, salt, and cinnamon. In another bowl, whisk together oil, eggs, applesauce, sugar, zucchini, and vanilla. Stir in flour mixture until just combined. Fold in chocolate. Divide batter evenly among prepared pans, filling each three-quarters full (about 1½ cups per pan).

Bake, rotating pans halfway through, until a tester inserted in centers of the loaves comes out clean, about 45 minutes. Let cool completely in pans on wire racks, then turn out bread. (Loaves can be tightly wrapped and kept at room temperature up to 2 days.)

You can also bake the batter in one 9-by-5-inch loaf pan for about 65 minutes.

Whole-Grain Pumpkin Bread

This may very well become your go-to recipe for the fall favorite, pumpkin bread. Finely ground pumpkin seeds are blended into the batter. MAKES ONE 9-INCH LOAF

Room-temperature butter, for pan

1 cup white whole-wheat flour

¾ cup all-purpose flour

1 teaspoon baking soda

¾ teaspoon coarse salt

¼ cup finely ground hulled pumpkin seeds (pepitas)

¼ teaspoon ground cinnamon

Pinch freshly grated nutmeg

Pinch ground cloves

Pinch ground allspice

1 cup canned unsweetened pumpkin puree

2 large eggs

½ cup safflower oil

⅓ cup buttermilk

1 teaspoon vanilla extract

½ cup natural cane sugar

½ cup packed dark brown sugar

Preheat oven to 350°F. Butter a 9-by-5-inch loaf pan. In a large bowl, whisk together both flours, baking soda, salt, ground pumpkin seeds, cinnamon, nutmeg, cloves, and allspice. In another bowl, stir together pumpkin puree, eggs, oil, buttermilk, vanilla, and both sugars until combined.

Pour pumpkin mixture into flour mixture, and fold with a flexible spatula until just combined (do not overmix). Transfer batter to prepared pan.

Bake, rotating pan halfway through, until top of bread springs back when gently pressed and a tester inserted into center of the loaf comes out clean, 50 to 60 minutes. (Tent with foil if browning too quickly.) Let cool in pan on a wire rack 20 minutes, then turn out bread and let cool completely. (Bread can be tightly wrapped and kept at room temperature up to 3 days.)

Molasses-Oat Bread

Oats pull double duty here: They're turned into a porridge and ground into a flour, helping create a molasses-sweetened loaf with a hearty texture and moist crumb. Try it at breakfast, toasted and spread with butter, or at lunch with any number of fillings (we like sliced turkey and cheddar). MAKES 1 ROUND LOAF

1½ cups plus 1 tablespoon old-fashioned rolled oats

1½ cups bread flour, plus more for dusting

1½ cups whole-wheat flour

¼ cup powdered nonfat dry milk

1½ cups plus 2 tablespoons water

¼ cup unsulfured molasses

1 envelope (¼ ounce) active dry yeast

¾ teaspoon coarse salt

Safflower oil, for brushing

1 large egg white, lightly beaten

In a saucepan, bring water just to a simmer. Pour the water over 1 cup oats in a bowl. Stir in molasses; let stand until mixture cools to warm, 10 minutes. Meanwhile, in a food processor coarsely grind ½ cup rolled oats. Transfer to bowl; add both flours and dry milk.

Sprinkle oat-molasses mixture with yeast. Stir in 1 cup flour mixture, and then the salt. Stir in remaining flour mixture, 1 cup at a time.

Turn dough out onto a floured surface. Using floured hands, knead until smooth, 5 to 10 minutes. Transfer dough to a lightly oiled bowl; turn to coat. Loosely cover with plastic wrap; let dough rise in a warm spot until doubled in bulk, 1 hour. Punch down dough. Transfer to a lightly floured surface. Knead dough once or twice. Flatten into a 9-inch circle.

Pull edges of dough up and in toward center; pinch to seal. Turn dough over. Pull down on dough with cupped hands to stretch top; pinch edges at bottom. Wrap hands around sides of dough; rotate to shape into a tight ball, 5½ inches in diameter and 3¾ inches high. Place on oiled baking sheet, seam side down. Cover with oiled plastic wrap. Let rise until dough doubles in bulk, 45 minutes to 1 hour.

Preheat oven to 400°F. Score an "X" in top of dough. Brush with egg white; sprinkle remaining oats. Bake 10 minutes. Reduce oven to 350°F. Bake, rotating sheet halfway through, until bottom sounds hollow when tapped, 40 to 45 minutes. Let cool completely on a wire rack before slicing.

5 Tips for Baking with Yeast

Many of the breads in this book rely on store-bought yeast, which is easier to use and requires less maintenance than a natural starter such as sourdough. Here, some suggestions for baking better loaves and rolls with commercial yeast.

1 Understand the different types.

There are three types of commercial yeast: active dry, instant (also known as quick rising), and fresh. Active dry yeast tends to be the most accessible; this granular yeast is usually dissolved in warm liquid before mixing with other ingredients. Instant yeast is milled into finer particles, dissolves more quickly, and works faster. (Active dry and instant yeast can be substituted one-for-one.) Some professional bakers prefer fresh yeast, which is sold refrigerated in cake form. It spoils within 2 weeks and can be hard to find, so we recommend it only if you bake bread often and know how to convert it easily.

2 Use the dough hook, or your hands.

The dough hook attachment on a stand mixer makes easy work of kneading dough. This helps develop the gluten and create the tighter, more regular crumb structure in breads like sandwich loaves, rolls, and sticky buns. (This is why artisan-style breads with an open crumb structure, like the one on page 248, are often not kneaded or kneaded very lightly.)

3 Choose low and slow.

Fermentation is the process in which yeast cells feed on bread's starches and release carbon dioxide (which causes bread to rise) and alcohol. The longer the fermentation, the less commercial yeast you have to use. Plus, long fermentation—whether at room temperature or the refrigerator—allows more good bacteria to form in the dough, which ultimately gives bread more flavor. At room temperature dough can rise for up to 18 hours; in the refrigerator, it can often rise as long as 3 days.

4 Give it a rest.

Gluten provides the necessary structure and texture for breads, but it also toughens up each time bread dough is handled and needs time to relax (otherwise the dough won't rise properly). After kneading, folding, or shaping dough, it must be left to rest at least 30 minutes before being handled again (or before baking).

5 Let your eyes guide you.

Yeast are living organisms that are more active when it's warm, so when deciding if it's time to go on to the next step of a recipe, use suggested times only as an estimate; visual clues are a much better guide.

Honey Whole-Wheat Bread

For the ultimate whole-wheat sandwich bread, this loaf relies on 100 percent whole-grain flour and equal amounts of honey and butter to keep it soft. The recipe is inspired by one from Ben Butler, the miller at Hayden Mills, an artisanal grain farm and mill in Queen Creek, Arizona. For the best-tasting loaf, look for fresh stone-ground whole-wheat bread flour. MAKES ONE 8½-INCH LOAF

- 3 tablespoons honey
- 1¾ cups warm water (about 110°F)
- 1 envelope (¼ ounce) active dry yeast (2¼ teaspoons)
- 4½ cups freshly milled whole-wheat bread flour, plus more for dusting
- 1 tablespoon coarse salt
- 3 tablespoons unsalted butter, melted, plus more for bowl and pan

In a small bowl, stir honey into warm water, then sprinkle with yeast. Let stand until foamy, about 5 minutes.

In a bowl, stir together flour and salt, then stir in yeast mixture and melted butter just until a dough forms. Knead on a lightly floured surface until smooth, 5 to 10 minutes. Transfer to a large buttered bowl, drape with plastic wrap, and let rise in a warm spot until dough doubles in bulk, about 45 minutes.

Preheat oven to 375°F. Butter a 9-by-5-inch loaf pan. Punch down dough. Shape into an 8-inch square, about 1 inch thick. Fold in two opposite sides to meet in the middle, overlapping slightly. Press seam to seal. Place dough seam side down in prepared pan. Sprinkle with flour. Drape with plastic wrap and let rise in a warm spot to ¾ inch above top of pan, 30 to 45 minutes.

Transfer pan to oven and immediately reduce heat to 350°F. Bake, rotating pan halfway through, until top is golden brown and bottom sounds hollow when tapped, 35 to 40 minutes. Let cool in pan on wire rack 20 minutes, then turn out bread onto rack and let cool completely. (Bread can be tightly wrapped and kept at room temperature up to 3 days or frozen up to 3 months.)

No-Knead Seeded Bread

Inspired by celebrated baker Jim Lahey's now-famous bread recipe, which first ran in the *New York Times* in 2006, this loaf develops its structure through a long, slow rise, without needing to knead. Like Lahey's bread, this loaf is baked in a Dutch oven to create a deeply browned crust. Whole-wheat flour, rolled oats, and a few handfuls of seeds are mixed into the dough and used to coat the outside of the loaf, so the bread is as healthy as it is flavorful. MAKES 1 ROUND LOAF

3 cups plus 3 tablespoons whole-wheat flour

2 cups unbleached bread flour

½ cup old-fashioned rolled oats

2 tablespoons coarse salt

1¼ teaspoons rapid rise (instant) yeast (½ envelope)

¼ cup plus 1 tablespoon hulled pumpkin seeds (pepitas)

3 tablespoons flaxseeds, preferably golden

3 tablespoons poppy seeds

3 tablespoons sesame seeds

¼ cup honey

2½ cups cold water

Extra-virgin olive oil, for drizzling

1 large egg white, lightly beaten

In a large bowl, stir together 3 cups whole-wheat flour, bread flour, oats, salt, yeast, ¼ cup pumpkin seeds, and 2 tablespoons each flax-, poppy, and sesame seeds. In a liquid measuring cup, whisk honey into the water, then stir into flour mixture until completely incorporated. Drizzle a thin layer of oil over top of dough, cover with plastic wrap, and refrigerate 2 hours; then let rise at room temperature 12 to 18 hours. (The longer it rises, the more flavor the bread will have.)

Coat inside of a large Dutch oven or lidded ovenproof pot with oil, and sprinkle evenly with 2 tablespoons whole-wheat flour. Stir dough to deflate, then quickly form into a ball and place in pot. Sprinkle with remaining 1 tablespoon whole-wheat flour and rub it over the dough. Brush top with egg white, and sprinkle with remaining 1 tablespoon each pumpkin, flax-, poppy, and sesame seeds. Cut an "X" in top of dough with a sharp knife. Cover and let rise in a warm spot until doubled in bulk, about 90 minutes.

Preheat oven to 475°F with a rack in lower third. Lightly sprinkle dough with water, cover pot, and place in oven. Reduce oven temperature to 450°F. Bake, rotating pot halfway through, until loaf is browned, about 45 minutes. Remove lid; bake 15 minutes more. Let cool in pot on a wire rack 15 minutes, then turn bread out on rack to cool completely. (Bread can be tightly wrapped and kept at room temperature up to 3 days.)

Gluten-Free Sandwich Bread

While its texture differs from wheat bread's, this gluten-free loaf has a delicious whole-grain flavor that will even appeal to those who don't follow a gluten-free diet. For the most satisfying bite, we suggest toasting before eating. You can also use this bread to make crumbs for coating chicken cutlets, fish, and sliced eggplant. Just slice, toast in a 350°F oven until dried, then grind. MAKES ONE 8½-INCH LOAF

2 tablespoons safflower oil, plus more for pan and plastic wrap

½ cup millet

1½ cups warm water (about 110°F)

1 cup brown rice flour

1 cup chickpea flour

½ cup tapioca flour

½ cup teff flour

2 envelopes (¼ ounce each) active dry yeast (2¼ teaspoons each)

2½ teaspoons xanthan gum

3 large eggs, room temperature

2 tablespoons unsulfured molasses

2 teaspoons coarse salt

Brush a 9-by-5-inch loaf pan with oil. In a small pan, combine millet and ½ cup warm water. Bring to a boil, remove from heat, and let stand 30 minutes.

Meanwhile, in the bowl of an electric mixer, whisk together flours, yeast, and xanthan gum. In another bowl, whisk together eggs, molasses, salt, and oil. Add egg mixture to dry ingredients. Using the paddle attachment, beat until combined. Beat in the remaining 1 cup warm water and the millet. Continue beating on medium-high for 5 minutes. (The mixture will be like thick, elastic cakey batter, not like traditional bread dough.)

Spread dough evenly in prepared pan. Lightly drape with oiled plastic wrap and place in a warm spot. Let rise until dough is about 1½ inches above edge of pan, about 1 hour 30 minutes. Once dough begins to dome, remove plastic for remainder of rising time.

Thirty minutes before you bake bread, preheat oven to 400°F. Transfer bread to oven, reduce temperature to 350°F, and bake, rotating pan halfway through, until dark brown and bottom sounds hollow when tapped, about 1 hour. Let cool in pan on a wire rack 20 minutes, then turn out bread onto rack to let cool completely, running a knife around the edge of the pan to loosen if necessary.

Whole-Wheat Stollen

In Germany, the holidays aren't complete without this sweet, dense, fruit-studded bread. To further enrich the flavor (and add a little more wholesomeness), this version incorporates whole-wheat pastry flour. Traditionally, the marzipan is kept in a single piece and encased in the loaf. Here it's crumbled first and sprinkled over the dough before baking. MAKES 2 LARGE LOAVES

- 3 cups unbleached bread flour, plus more for dusting
- 2½ cups whole-wheat pastry flour
- ¼ cup plus 2 tablespoons natural cane sugar
- ½ teaspoon coarse salt
- ¼ teaspoon ground mace
- ¼ teaspoon freshly grated nutmeg
- 1 envelope (¼ ounce) active dry yeast (2¼ teaspoons)
- 1 cup milk, warmed (about 110°F)
- ¼ cup warm water (about 110°F)
- 1 stick (½ cup) plus 2 tablespoons unsalted butter, melted; plus more, room temperature, for brushing
- 3 large eggs, lightly beaten
- 1½ cups golden raisins, soaked in ¼ cup orange juice and drained
- 1½ cups dried currants, soaked in ¼ cup cognac and drained
- ⅓ cup dried apricots, finely chopped
- ⅓ cup candied orange peel, finely chopped
- 1 cup almonds, coarsely chopped
- Finely grated zest of 1 lemon
- 7 ounces marzipan
- Superfine sugar, for dusting

In the bowl of a stand mixer fitted with a dough hook, combine both flours, granulated sugar, salt, mace, nutmeg, and yeast. Stir in milk, water, and 1 stick melted butter. Add eggs and knead on low until dough looks fairly smooth, about 4 minutes. Add the dried fruits, candied fruit, almonds, and lemon zest and continue kneading until evenly incorporated, 6 minutes.

Transfer dough to a buttered bowl, cover with plastic wrap, and let rise in a warm place until doubled in bulk, 1 to 2 hours.

Punch down dough and divide into 2 equal pieces. Roll each piece into a 12-by-8-inch rectangle. Working with one rectangle at a time, brush each with 1 tablespoon melted butter. Crumble half of the marzipan and scatter it evenly down the center of dough. Fold one long side to the center, then fold the other long side over first side, overlapping it by 1 inch. Repeat with remaining dough and marzipan.

Turn loaves over, taper the ends, and place on 2 parchment-lined baking sheets, seam sides down. Cover loaves with plastic wrap and let rise again in a warm spot, 1 to 1½ hours.

Preheat oven to 350°F. Bake loaves, rotating sheets halfway through, until golden brown, 35 to 40 minutes. Brush all over with butter and sprinkle generously with superfine sugar. Let cool completely on sheets. (Loaves can be tightly wrapped and kept at room temperature up to 1 week.)

Hazelnut Hot-Cross Buns

Thanks to the addition of hazelnut flour, these traditional Easter breads are richer than usual. Per the name, the buns are delicious warm, but the flavor improves after the buns stand at room temperature for a few hours. MAKES 24

- 1 cup milk, warmed (about 110°F)

- 2 envelopes (¼ ounce each) active dry yeast (4½ teaspoons)

- ½ cup natural cane sugar

- 2 teaspoons coarse salt

- 1½ sticks (¾ cup) unsalted butter, melted and cooled, plus more for bowl and pan

- ¾ teaspoon ground cinnamon

- 4 large eggs, lightly beaten

- 1 cup hazelnut flour

- 4½ cups plus 2 tablespoons all-purpose flour, plus more for dusting

- 1 cup chopped dried cherries

- 1 large egg, beaten with 1 teaspoon water

  Double recipe Drizzly Glaze (see page 287)

For piping, transfer glaze to a resealable plastic bag and snip off corner.

Pour warm milk into bowl of a stand mixer fitted with a dough hook. With mixer on low, add yeast, cane sugar, salt, butter, cinnamon, and eggs. Add hazelnut flour and 4½ cups all-purpose flour, 1 cup at a time, and mix until a soft, slightly sticky dough forms, 3 minutes (if it seems too sticky, add up to 2 more tablespoons flour). Continue kneading, scraping down hook and sides of bowl until smooth, 4 minutes longer. Add cherries, and knead until just combined, 30 seconds.

Turn out dough onto a floured surface. Knead about 1 minute. Shape dough into a ball, and place in a buttered bowl, turning to coat. Cover bowl tightly with plastic wrap. Let dough rise in a warm spot until doubled in bulk, 1 hour 20 minutes, or refrigerate overnight.

Generously butter an 11-by-17-inch baking sheet. Turn out dough onto work surface and knead briefly. Divide dough into 24 pieces, about 2 ounces each. Shape pieces into tight balls, and space ½ inch apart on baking sheet. Cover with plastic wrap, and let rise in a warm spot until doubled in bulk, 45 minutes to 1 hour.

Preheat oven to 375°F. Brush tops of buns with egg wash; using a buttered knife, slice a cross into each. Bake, rotating pan halfway through, until buns are golden brown, about 25 minutes. Transfer pan to a wire rack to cool. Pipe the glaze over each bun and serve.

Honey-Wheat Parker House Rolls

Beloved buttery Parker House rolls are made more wholesome with the addition of whole-wheat flour. For the best flavor, make the dough the night before, then assemble and bake soon before serving. This recipe can be easily doubled. MAKES 15

---

1 cup warm water (about 110°F)

1 envelope (¼ ounce) active dry yeast (2¼ teaspoons)

3 tablespoons honey

1 large egg

1¾ cups whole-wheat flour

1¾ cups all-purpose flour, plus more for dusting

2 teaspoons coarse salt

1 stick (½ cup) unsalted butter, room temperature, plus more for pan

Flaky salt, such as Maldon, for sprinkling

In the bowl of a stand mixer fitted with a dough hook, combine water, yeast, honey, and egg; let stand 5 minutes until foamy. In another bowl, whisk together the flours and salt.

Add the flour mixture to the water mixture, and knead on low until dough is smooth and elastic, about 5 minutes. Add 4 tablespoons of butter, 1 tablespoon at a time, and continue kneading until fully incorporated, about 4 minutes.

Shape the dough into a ball and return to mixer bowl. Cover with plastic wrap and let rest in a warm spot, 30 minutes. Transfer dough to refrigerator and let rise 8 hours or up to 18 hours.

Generously butter an 8-inch square pan. Melt remaining 4 tablespoons butter. Turn dough out onto a floured work surface. Roll into an 18-inch square. Using a sharp knife, cut dough into 3 equal strips lengthwise and 5 equal strips crosswise (you will have 15 rectangles). Fold each rectangle in half, and place in prepared baking pan, 3 across and 5 down, overlapping slightly. Brush tops evenly with 2 tablespoons melted butter. Cover pan with buttered plastic wrap. Let rise until dough does not spring back when pressed, 25 to 30 minutes.

Preheat oven to 375°F. Bake, rotating pan halfway through, until rolls are deeply golden, about 22 minutes. Brush with remaining 2 tablespoons butter and sprinkle with flaky salt. Serve warm.

Stuffed Whole-Wheat Flatbreads

Consider these a simpler take on paratha, the Indian flatbread. Traditionally, paratha is slightly puffy and layered because it is brushed with ghee (clarified butter) and folded several times; this version gets a lift from baking powder. Stuff with the curried vegetables here, or try an equal amount of mashed potatoes or sweet potatoes in place of the cauliflower. SERVES 6

For the flatbreads

- 2 cups whole-wheat flour
- ½ teaspoon baking powder
- 1 teaspoon coarse salt
- 3 tablespoons extra-virgin olive oil, plus more for brushing
- ½ cup warm water (about 110°F)

For the filling

- ½ head cauliflower, cut into large florets (about 3 cups)
- 1 tablespoon extra-virgin olive oil
- ½ teaspoon cumin seeds
- 1 teaspoon ground coriander
- ½ teaspoon ground turmeric
- 6 cups baby spinach, chopped
- ½ cup fresh or thawed frozen peas
- Coarse salt

Make the flatbreads: In a bowl, stir together flour, baking powder, and salt. Stir in oil and warm water until combined. Turn out dough onto a work surface and knead until it's smooth and springs back when pressed, 5 minutes. Cover with an inverted bowl and let rest 30 minutes.

Meanwhile, make the filling: In a saucepan with a steamer insert, steam cauliflower until very soft, 8 to 10 minutes, then transfer to a bowl and mash with a fork. Heat oil in a skillet over medium and toast cumin until fragrant, about 30 seconds, then stir in coriander and turmeric. Stir in spinach and cook until just wilted. Remove mixture from heat and stir in mashed cauliflower and the peas. Season with salt.

Divide dough into 6 balls, and roll out each to an 8-inch round. Heat a cast-iron skillet over medium and cook rounds, one at a time, until slightly puffed and golden, 1 to 2 minutes. Flip and spread half of each round with filling. Gently fold over other half, and cook until golden, 2 minutes. Flip and cook 2 minutes more. Brush the top with oil. Cut flatbreads in half and serve.

Whole-Wheat Pita Bread

This staple of Middle Eastern and Mediterranean cuisines is easy to make. It starts with a simple yeast dough (we used a mix of whole-wheat flour and all-purpose white) and bakes in a very hot oven. The heat activates the yeast and creates steam, causing the dough to puff up dramatically, forming the signature pocket. MAKES 16

4½ cups all-purpose flour, plus more for dusting

2 envelopes (¼ ounce each) active dry yeast (2¼ teaspoons each)

1 tablespoon honey

2¼ cups warm water (about 110°F)

1½ cups whole-wheat flour

1 tablespoon coarse salt

⅓ cup extra-virgin olive oil, plus more for bowl

Fine cornmeal, for sprinkling

For extra-flavorful pita, brush one side of each dough round with olive oil and sprinkle with za'atar, a Middle Eastern blend of thyme, sesame seeds, and sumac, before baking.

In a large bowl, whisk together 1 cup all-purpose flour, yeast, honey, and 1 cup warm water until smooth. Cover with plastic wrap; let rise in a warm spot until doubled in bulk, about 30 minutes. Stir in remaining 3½ cups all-purpose flour, the whole-wheat flour, salt, oil, and remaining 1¼ cups warm water.

Transfer dough to a floured surface. Knead dough, dusting hands and surface with more flour as needed, until smooth and elastic, 10 minutes. Transfer to an oiled bowl, turning to coat. Cover and let rise again until doubled in bulk, 45 minutes.

Punch down dough, and form into a ball; then turn out onto a floured surface. Quarter dough. Working with one piece at a time (drape a kitchen towel over the rest), divide each quarter into 4 pieces. Roll each piece into a ball and pinch, tightening the ball. Turn pinched-side down, flatten with your palm, and roll into a 6-inch round. Transfer rounds to rimmed baking sheets sprinkled with cornmeal; drape with kitchen towels and repeat with the remaining dough. Let rest 30 minutes.

Preheat oven to 500°F and set an inverted rimmed baking sheet on rack in lowest position. Place 4 dough rounds on preheated sheet. Bake until puffed, 2 minutes. Flip and bake until golden in spots and just cooked through, 1 minute more. Transfer to a basket lined with a kitchen towel; cover to keep warm. Bake remaining pitas and serve.

Spelt Tortillas

Homemade flour tortillas are remarkably tastier than store-bought. Spelt flour brings whole-grain's virtue but creates a softer result. These tortillas work well for tacos, or you can use them to make a sweet treat: Spread with your favorite nut butter, top with bananas, and drizzle with honey. MAKES 12

3 cups spelt flour, plus more for dusting

¾ teaspoon baking powder

1 teaspoon coarse salt

½ cup plus 1 tablespoon sour cream

1 cup buttermilk

If you prefer, you can use Kamut flour in place of the spelt. It has a naturally buttery flavor and will make the tortillas a little chewier.

In a bowl, combine flour, baking powder, and salt. Add sour cream and buttermilk, and mix with your hands until a dough forms. Turn onto a lightly floured surface, and knead until dough is smooth and springs back when pressed, 5 minutes. Cover with plastic wrap, and let rest for 30 minutes.

Divide dough evenly into 12 pieces. Using a lightly floured rolling pin, roll each piece into an 8-inch round, less than ⅛ inch thick. Place rounds on a parchment-lined baking sheet, layering parchment between each to prevent sticking. Cover with parchment, then with a damp kitchen towel. Let rest for 30 minutes (or cover and refrigerate overnight).

Heat a cast-iron skillet over medium. Working with one piece at a time, cook dough, turning once, until brown spots appear, about 2 minutes per side. Transfer to a plate, and cover with parchment and then a damp towel. Serve warm. (Tortillas can be frozen between layers of parchment in a resealable plastic bag up to 1 month. Thaw at room temperature.)

Whole-Wheat Popovers

Made with a combination of all-purpose and whole-wheat flours, these pleasantly sturdy popovers are perfect with eggs for breakfast, or as an accompaniment to soup. A standard popover tin has straight sides and plenty of space around each cup to give batter the best chance to rise high. If you don't have one, grease and fill 6 outer cups of a muffin tin and reduce the baking time by 5 minutes. MAKES 6

¾ cup whole-wheat flour

¾ cup all-purpose flour

1¼ teaspoons coarse salt

3 large eggs, room temperature

1½ cups milk, room temperature

Safflower oil, for pan

It's important that the eggs and milk are at room temperature before you proceed with the recipe. To heat eggs quickly, submerge them in warm water for 10 minutes; for milk, warm quickly on the stovetop.

Preheat oven to 450°F with a nonstick popover pan on rack in lowest position. In a bowl, whisk together both flours and salt.

In a large bowl, whisk together eggs and milk until very frothy, about 1 minute. Whisk flour mixture into egg mixture just until batter is the consistency of heavy cream with some small lumps remaining.

Remove popover pan from oven and quickly brush with oil. Dividing evenly, fill popover cups (about three-quarters full) with batter. Bake 20 minutes, then reduce oven temperature to 350°F. Continue baking until popovers are golden brown and dry to the touch, about 20 minutes more; do not open the oven as they bake. Immediately turn out popovers onto a wire rack (they lose their crunch if they linger in pan). Poke a small opening in the side of each with a paring knife to let steam escape. Serve immediately.

Seeded English Muffins

These morning favorites rely on a poolish (also known as a sponge or pre-ferment), a portion of dough that rises overnight before the ingredients are added. This method gives the muffins a complex, yeasty quality and creates impressively craggy interiors. MAKES ABOUT 12

2¼ cups whole-wheat flour

1 envelope (¼ ounce) active dry yeast (2¼ teaspoons)

1 cup warm water (about 110°F)

1 cup all-purpose flour, plus more for dusting

1½ teaspoons coarse salt

1 tablespoon sesame seeds

1 teaspoon poppy seeds

1 teaspoon caraway seeds

¾ cup milk

Medium-grind cornmeal, for dusting

Safflower oil, for frying

To form the poolish, stir together 1¼ cups whole-wheat flour, ½ teaspoon yeast, and the warm water in a large bowl. In another bowl, stir together remaining 1 cup whole-wheat flour, the all-purpose flour, remaining 1¾ teaspoons yeast, the salt, and seeds. Sprinkle on top of batter but do not stir in. Cover with plastic wrap and let stand at room temperature overnight.

The next day, add milk to bowl and stir to form a soft dough. Cover with plastic and let rise 90 minutes; every 20 minutes during the first hour, gently fold dough from four different points toward the center with a bowl scraper or oiled fingers.

Preheat oven to 350°F. Sprinkle a work surface and a parchment-lined baking sheet with cornmeal. Gently turn dough out, and press into a 10-inch square, about ¾ inch thick, deflating dough as little as possible. Cut rounds with a floured 3¼-inch biscuit cutter. Transfer rounds to prepared baking sheet, and let rest 10 minutes. Gently form scraps into a ball; cover, and let rest 15 minutes, then press and cut more rounds.)

Heat a 10-inch straight-sided skillet over medium. Lightly oil pan and fry muffins, 4 at a time, turning over, until golden brown, 2 to 3 minutes per side. Return muffins to sheet pan. Bake until just cooked through, about 8 minutes. Transfer to wire racks and let cool completely. (Muffins can be frozen in a resealable bag up to 1 month.)

Whole-Grain Seeded Wafer Crackers

These thin, almost lacy crackers feature four flavorful types of seeds, as well as rye and wheat flours. Serve them alongside any salad or soup, or as a nice addition to a cheese plate. MAKES 16

1¼ cups warm water (about 110°F)

1 tablespoon rapid rise (instant) yeast (from two ¼-ounce packages)

1 tablespoon cumin seeds

2 cups all-purpose flour, plus more for dusting

¾ cup rye flour

½ cup whole-wheat flour

⅓ cup nigella seeds

⅓ cup sesame seeds

⅓ cup flaxseeds

2 teaspoons coarse salt

Nigella seeds add a distinctive oniony flavor, but if you can't find them, use black sesame seeds instead.

In the bowl of a stand mixer fitted with a dough hook, whisk together water and yeast. Add remaining ingredients. Knead on medium until dough is smooth and slightly sticky, about 7 minutes. Cover bowl with plastic wrap and let rise in a warm spot until almost doubled in bulk, about 1 hour.

Preheat oven to 425°F. Turn out dough onto a lightly floured surface and pat into a 1-inch-thick square. Cut into 16 equal pieces, then shape each into a ball, keeping other balls covered as you work.

Working with one piece at a time and using a small amount of flour, flatten each ball with your hands; then roll out as thinly as possible to about the thickness of the seeds (shapes will be irregular). Transfer each piece to a parchment-lined baking sheet, 2 to a sheet. Use a fork to prick all over.

Bake in batches, flipping each cracker over halfway through, until golden on edges, about 20 minutes per batch. Using tongs, transfer crackers to wire racks and let cool completely before serving. (Crackers can be kept in an airtight container at room temperature up to 1 month.)

Rye Soft Pretzels

Pretzels get their bronzed and pleasantly bitter exteriors from a quick poach in a baking soda solution, which hastens the browning as they bake. Rye flour's sweet maltiness is perfect for pretzels; the only things you need to serve alongside are cold beers and an assortment of mustards and dips. MAKES 1 DOZEN

- 2 cups warm water (about 110°F)

- 1 tablespoons plus 1 teaspoon honey

- 1 teaspoon active dry yeast (from one ¼ ounce envelope)

- 3½ cups all-purpose flour, plus more as needed

- 2 cups rye flour

- 1 tablespoon coarse salt

- 2 teaspoons unsalted butter, melted, plus more for baking sheets

- ½ cup baking soda

- 1 large egg, lightly beaten

  Pretzel or coarse salt, for sprinkling

  Anise seed, sesame seeds, caraway seeds, and poppy seeds, for sprinkling

In the bowl of a stand mixer fitted with a dough hook, combine water and honey. Sprinkle with yeast, and let stand until foamy, 10 minutes.

In a large bowl, whisk 3 cups all-purpose flour, rye flour, and salt. Add 1 cup of flour mixture to yeast, and knead on low until combined. Add the remaining 4 cups flour mixture, 1 cup at a time, and knead until combined, about 30 seconds. Knead on medium-low until dough pulls away from sides of bowl, about 1½ minutes. Add the remaining ½ cup all-purpose flour, and knead on low until dough is smooth, soft, and elastic, about 6 minutes more.

Pour melted butter into a large bowl; swirl to coat sides. Transfer dough to bowl, turning dough to completely cover all sides with butter. Cover with plastic wrap and refrigerate overnight.

Remove the dough from the refrigerator and leave in a warm spot until dough has doubled in size, 1 to 3 hours.

Butter 2 large rimmed baking sheets. Punch down dough to remove any air bubbles. Transfer to a very lightly floured work surface. Pat into a rectangle and cut the dough into 12 equal pieces (about 3½ ounces each).

Working with one piece at a time and keeping the others covered lightly with plastic, roll the dough into an 18-inch-long rope. Make a "U" shape with the rope and cross the ends over, pinching them at the bottom of the "U" to form a pretzel. Transfer to one of the prepared baking sheets, cover with a kitchen towel, and repeat process with remaining dough, dividing them between the 2 sheets. Let pretzels rest until they rise slightly, about 15 minutes.

Meanwhile, preheat oven to 450°F. Fill a large, wide pot with water (about 10 minutes); bring to a boil and add baking soda.

Reduce water to a simmer and add 3 or 4 pretzels. Poach for 30 seconds. Use a slotted spoon or a spider to return pretzels to baking sheets. Poach remaining pretzels.

Brush pretzels with beaten egg. Sprinkle evenly with salt and seeds. Bake, rotating baking sheets halfway through, until golden brown, 12 to 15 minutes. Let cool on wire rack, or eat warm. (Pretzels are best the day they're made, but can be lightly covered and kept at room temperature up to 2 days.)

Mustard Dip

Martha endearingly refers to this recipe as Brooke's Mustard Dip, in honor of the woman who created it during their catering days.

———————

Combine ½ cup dry mustard, ¾ cup distilled white vinegar, and ½ cup white wine or dry vermouth in a nonreactive bowl. Cover and let stand overnight.

In another nonreactive bowl, whisk 3 large eggs with ½ cup natural cane sugar and 1½ teaspoons coarse salt until very light and foamy, about 3 minutes. Add mustard mixture and cook over a pot of simmering water, whisking occasionally, until thick, about 1 hour. Let cool slightly; then refrigerate, covered, until ready to use.

Just before baking, sprinkle each pretzel with salt and one type of seed—or try a combination of seeds, "everything" style.

Whole-Wheat Monkey Bread

The same whole-wheat dough used for the Seeded Breakfast Rolls on page 57 and the Honey-Wheat Parker House Rolls on page 257 is transformed into a sweet pull-apart treat that's as fun to make as it is to eat. MAKES ONE 10-INCH LOAF

For the dough

- 1 cup warm water (about 110°F)
- 1 envelope (¼ ounce) active dry yeast (2¼ teaspoons)
- 3 tablespoons honey
- 1 large egg
- 1¾ cups whole-wheat flour
- 1¾ cups all-purpose flour
- 2 teaspoons coarse salt
- 4 tablespoons unsalted butter, room temperature

For the topping

- 1 stick (½ cup) unsalted butter, melted, plus more for pan
- 1½ cups packed light brown sugar
- 1 tablespoon plus 1 teaspoon ground cinnamon

Feel free to switch up the spiced sugar, adding a pinch of cardamom or ground ginger along with the cinnamon.

Make the dough: In the bowl of an electric mixer fitted with a dough hook, combine the water, yeast, honey, and egg; let stand 5 minutes, until foamy. In another bowl, whisk together both flours and the salt. Add the flour mixture to the water mixture, and knead on low until dough is smooth and elastic, 5 minutes. Add butter, 1 tablespoon at a time, and knead until incorporated, 4 minutes.

Shape dough into a ball and return to the mixer bowl. Cover with plastic wrap and let rest in a warm spot, 30 minutes. Transfer dough to refrigerator and let rise 8 hours or up to 18 hours.

Make the topping: Generously butter a 10-inch Bundt pan. In a small bowl, combine ¾ cup brown sugar and 2 teaspoons cinnamon. In another bowl, combine melted butter and remaining ¾ cup sugar and 2 teaspoons cinnamon.

Break off 1-inch pieces of dough and roll into balls. Roll in sugar mixture, and layer on top of each other in prepared pan. Drizzle with melted butter mixture. Cover with plastic wrap and let rise in warm place until doubled in bulk, about 1 hour.

Preheat oven to 350°F. Bake, rotating pan halfway through until bread feels firm when pressed lightly and is dark golden brown, 30 to 35 minutes. Let cool in pan 5 minutes, then invert onto serving plate and cool 20 minutes more. (If any pieces stick, just pull them out and arrange them back in place.) Serve warm.

Coconut-Pumpkin Bread Pudding

Pumpkin puree and warming spices flavor this cozy autumnal dessert. Coconut milk is the secret to the dairy-free custard, which gets a delicious crackly top from a simple caramel that hardens as it cools. SERVES 8

For the pudding

Coconut oil or unsalted butter, room temperature, for dish

1 (10-ounce) day-old whole-wheat seed loaf, cut into ½-inch cubes (6 cups)

1 can (15 ounces) unsweetened pumpkin puree

1 can (15 ounces) coconut milk

3 large eggs, lightly beaten

¾ cup raw sugar, such as turbinado

½ teaspoon coarse salt

1 teaspoon vanilla extract

1 teaspoon ground cinnamon

½ teaspoon ground ginger

¼ cup water

For the topping

¼ cup plus 2 tablespoons natural cane sugar

3 tablespoons water

Make the bread pudding: Preheat oven to 200°F. Oil or butter a 2-quart baking dish. Spread out bread cubes in a single layer on a baking sheet and bake until dry and just beginning to turn golden, about 25 minutes.

Increase oven temperature to 350°F. In a large bowl, whisk together pumpkin puree, coconut milk, eggs, turbinado sugar, salt, vanilla, cinnamon, ginger, and water. Arrange toasted bread in dish. Pour custard over bread and stir to coat. Let stand 10 minutes. Bake until custard is golden-brown and springs back when pressed, about 50 minutes. Transfer pan to wire rack and let cool slightly.

Make the topping: In a small saucepan, combine cane sugar with water. Cook over medium heat, stirring occasionally, until sugar dissolves and syrup comes to a boil. Stop stirring and continue cooking, swirling pan occasionally, until amber, 10 to 12 minutes. Drizzle caramel over pudding and let cool until caramel has hardened. Serve warm.

The Basics

Confectioners' Sugar

You can start with your favorite type of granulated sugar, including organic varieties and even coconut sugar. Cornstarch is optional, but it helps keep the powdered sugar from clumping. MAKES ABOUT ½ CUP

1 cup granulated sugar

1 teaspoon cornstarch (optional)

In a blender or food processor, combine sugar and cornstarch, if using, and pulse until it reaches a powdery consistency, about 1 minute. Sift confectioners' sugar before using. (Store in an airtight container at room temperature up to 1 year.)

Baking Powder

If you're out of baking powder, or it's no longer effective (test by adding 1 teaspoon to one-half cup water and seeing if it fizzes), you can make your own in a pinch. Be aware that this mixture is single-acting; it starts reacting as soon as it comes into contact with moisture, so you must get your batters into the oven right away. Double-acting baking powders—the types you usually buy at the supermarket—use ingredients that react first when they come in contact with moisture, and then again during baking. MAKES 3 TABLESPOONS

2 tablespoons cream of tartar

1 tablespoon baking soda

In a small bowl, mix cream of tartar and baking soda. Sift baking powder before using. (Store in an airtight container at room temperature up to 6 weeks.)

Buttermilk

Buttermilk creates exceptionally tender baked goods. This curdled milk mixture doesn't taste the same as commercial cultured buttermilk, but it works cup-for-cup in baking recipes that call for buttermilk. MAKES ABOUT 1 CUP

1 cup whole milk

1 tablespoon lemon juice or apple cider vinegar

In a liquid measuring cup, stir milk with lemon juice. Let stand until curdled, about 10 minutes, before using.

Vanilla Extract

Vanilla extract couldn't be easier to make: You simply infuse liquor with the beans for at least 1 month; the results keep indefinitely. Store the extract in your pantry or funnel into small bottles for gifting. MAKES 1 CUP

2 vanilla beans

1 cup vodka or bourbon

Split vanilla beans lengthwise, and place in a resealable jar or bottle. Cover with vodka. Seal and store in a cool place, shaking occasionally, for 1 to 2 months before using. (You can leave vanilla beans in the jar or bottle, topping off with more vodka as you use the extract.)

Nut Butter

Nut butter takes no more than 10 minutes to prepare, and making your own allows you to control the amounts of salt and sugar, if any, you use. While adding oil is not necessary, it does produce butters with a creamier consistency. MAKES 1 CUP

2 cups shelled unsalted nuts, including pecans, peanuts, skinned hazelnuts, or cashews, toasted if desired (see page 288)

1 to 2 tablespoons safflower oil

Brown sugar and salt, to taste (optional)

In a food processor, combine nuts and 1 tablespoon oil, and process until creamy, stopping occasionally to scrape down the sides. Add up to 1 tablespoon more oil, 1 teaspoon at a time, for a creamier butter. Add brown sugar and salt, as desired, and process to incorporate. (Butter can be refrigerated for up to 1 week; stir before using.)

Nut Milk

Homemade nut milk can be a revelation: It's so much more flavorful than the store-bought type. With a blender, a fine-mesh sieve, nuts, and water, you can whip up an entire quart in just a few minutes (after you soak the nuts). Soaking the nuts overnight produces the creamiest milk. MAKES ABOUT 1 QUART

1 cup raw nuts, such as almonds, cashews, pistachios, or skinned hazelnuts

4 cups room-temperature water, plus more for soaking

Place nuts in a bowl and cover with an inch of water; refrigerate overnight. Drain and rinse nuts. Transfer nuts to a blender and add 4 cups of water; blend until pureed and frothy. Strain nut puree through a fine-mesh sieve lined with cheesecloth, pressing down on solids. Compost the solids, or add up to ¼ cup to muffin or pancake batter. (Milk can be refrigerated up to 5 days; shake before using.)

Coconut Milk

Opening a coconut and prying out the meat takes a little persistence and strength, but the results are worth it. You can use this coconut milk in place of any unsweetened full-fat coconut milk. MAKES ABOUT 2 CUPS

1 fresh, mature coconut

1½ cups warm water

Much like nut pulp, you can use the coconut pulp in simple baked goods. Because it's so fiber-rich and dense, start by adding 2 tablespoons of it to your favorite muffin, pancake, and quickbread recipes, increasing from there, as desired.

Preheat oven to 375°F. Using a screwdriver or metal skewer, poke the three indentations (the "eyes") at end of coconut to find the soft one; make a hole in coconut. Drain coconut water and discard. Put coconut in oven for 15 to 20 minutes. Remove from oven and let stand until cool.

Wrap coconut in a kitchen towel, and use a meat mallet or hammer to crack open. Use a butter knife to pry meat out of shell.

With a vegetable peeler, remove the dark brown skin. Cut meat into 1-inch pieces and transfer to a blender. Add the warm water to blender, and blend on high for 1 to 2 minutes, until very thick and frothy.

Strain coconut milk through a fine-mesh sieve lined with cheesecloth, pressing down on the solids with a flexible spatula. (Compost the solids, or reserve for another use; see tip at left). Add a little coconut water if you would like a thinner coconut milk. (Coconut milk can be refrigerated up to 5 days; shake before using.)

Yogurt

Making your own may sound ambitious, but it's really not: It takes only two ingredients, some common kitchen equipment, and about 20 minutes of hands-on time. Free of stabilizers and sweeteners, the resulting yogurt is remarkably silky, clean tasting, and mild. MAKES ABOUT 1 QUART

---

1 **quart milk**

3 **tablespoons plain yogurt**

For Greek-style yogurt, strain the yogurt in a cheesecloth-lined sieve for 2 to 4 hours.

In a large saucepan, heat milk on medium-high until it reaches 180°F, stirring occasionally to prevent scorching, 5 to 7 minutes. Let cool to 115°F.

In a bowl, whisk together 1 cup warmed milk and the yogurt. Stir into remaining milk until completely blended.

Transfer to a clean 1-quart mason jar. Wrap jar (without lid) in two clean kitchen towels, completely covering sides and top. Let stand undisturbed in a warm place until yogurt reaches consistency of custard, 4 hours for a thinner, milder yogurt or 5 hours for a thicker, tangier one.

Refrigerate uncovered jar; when it's cool to the touch, about 30 minutes, screw on a tight-fitting lid. (Yogurt can be refrigerated up to 1 week.)

Ricotta

This may be an uncomplicated cheese, but it's far from plain. You can make your own simply by cooking milk and cream, adding a little lemon juice, and letting the result drain in cheesecloth. We love ricotta in cheesecake (like the one on page 212) and tart fillings (page 166). MAKES 2¾ CUPS

- 2 quarts whole milk
- 1½ cups best-quality heavy cream
- 1 teaspoon coarse salt
- ¼ cup fresh lemon juice (from 2 lemons), strained to remove pulp

Use the whey in place of buttermilk in simple baked goods, such as muffins, or add it in place of some of the water in yeast breads. You can also freeze it in ice-cube trays and use in smoothies, or simply enjoy it as is, poured over ice.

Line a mesh colander with a triple layer of cheesecloth and place inside a deeper, slightly larger bowl. In a 4- to 5-quart pot, combine milk, cream, and salt. Warm mixture over medium-high heat, stirring frequently with a wooden spoon to prevent scorching, until it reaches 195°F on an instant thermometer, about 15 minutes.

Add lemon juice, stirring gently until just combined. Remove pot from heat and let stand 5 minutes. (The combination of the acid and the residual heat will cause the milk to coagulate, or curdle, separating into a soft mass, curds, and a cloudy liquid, whey.)

Gently pour curds and whey into the prepared colander. Let mixture stand, pouring off whey occasionally, until most of whey has drained from still-wet curds, 20 minutes.

Gather up ricotta in cheesecloth, and turn it out into a bowl. For a denser ricotta, which can be preferable for baking, hang it to drain for another hour. Repurpose whey (see tip, at left) or discard it. (Ricotta is best the day it's made, but can be refrigerated in an airtight container up to 4 days.)

Squash Puree

In the fall, farmers' markets brim with different varieties of winter squash. Our three favorites for baking are the delicately nutty and mild acorn, silky and sweet butternut, and dense and earthy Kabocha. You can use squash puree in place of canned pumpkin in recipes for pies, cakes, and scones. MAKES ABOUT 2 CUPS

2   pounds squash, such as 1 or 2 acorn, cut into 2-inch wedges and seeded; or 1 or 2 medium butternut, peeled, cut into 2-inch cubes, and seeded; or ½ Kabocha, cut into 2-inch wedges and seeded

In a large pot fitted with a steamer basket (or colander), bring 2 inches water to a boil. Add squash. Cover and steam until soft, 15 to 20 minutes. Let cool completely. If using acorn or Kabocha, scoop out flesh and discard skins.

Puree steamed squash in a food processor until smooth. If using Kabocha, add ¼ cup water before processing, then adjust until consistency is smooth. (Puree can be refrigerated up to 3 days or frozen up to 1 month; thaw in refrigerator before using.)

Applesauce

McIntosh apples give applesauce that classic flavor, but a mix of varieties adds dimension. MAKES 6 CUPS

4   pounds apples, such as McIntosh, Gala, and Braeburn, peeled, cored, and sliced

¼   cup fresh lemon juice (from 2 lemons)

1½   cups water

In a large pot, bring apples, lemon juice, and water to a boil over high. Reduce heat and simmer until apples are very soft and falling apart, 25 to 30 minutes.

Mash with a potato masher or pulse in a food processor until smooth. Let cool, then transfer applesauce to airtight containers. (Applesauce can be refrigerated up to 5 days or frozen up to 2 months; thaw in refrigerator before using.)

GLAZES AND FROSTINGS

Caramel Drizzle

¼ cup sugar

1 teaspoon water

In a small saucepan, heat sugar with the water over medium-high. Cook, without stirring, until sugar at edges begins to melt and turn clear, about 3 minutes. Continue to cook, swirling pan often, until medium amber throughout, 1½ to 2 minutes. Use immediately.

Cream Cheese Frosting

16 ounces (2 bars) cream cheese

1 stick (½ cup) unsalted butter, room temperature

2 cups confectioners' sugar

1 teaspoon vanilla extract

¼ teaspoon coarse salt

In a bowl, with an electric mixer, beat cream cheese with butter until fluffy, about 5 minutes. Add confectioners' sugar, 1 cup at a time, and beat until smooth, scraping down sides of bowl as necessary. Beat in vanilla and salt. Makes enough for three 8- or 9-inch-round cake layers or 3 dozen cupcakes.

Drizzly Glaze

1 cup confectioners' sugar

2 tablespoons milk

In a small bowl, whisk together confectioners' sugar with 1 tablespoon milk until smooth. Add more milk as needed, a drop at a time (up to 1 tablespoon), to loosen glaze. Use a spoon to drizzle glaze over cookies and scones, or dip cupcakes directly in glaze. Let set for at least 10 minutes.

Chocolate Ganache Frosting

3 ounces bittersweet chocolate, finely chopped

½ cup heavy cream

Put chocolate in a bowl. In a small saucepan, heat cream until just simmering. Pour cream over chocolate and let stand 10 minutes; then stir until smooth. Let stand, stirring occasionally, until thickened and spreadable, about 1 hour.

TECHNIQUES

MEASURING DRY INGREDIENTS

Measure dry ingredients (including flour and sugar) and semisolid ingredients (such as peanut butter) in graduated dry measuring cups. For flour, first whisk it to aerate it, then spoon the flour into the cup and fill to overflowing; finish by leveling with a straightedge such as an offset spatula. (Never shake the cup or tap it on the counter to level; both will lead to inaccurate measurements.) If a recipe calls for "sifted flour," sift the flour first, and then measure it; if it calls for "flour, sifted," measure first and then sift. When measuring brown sugar, pack firmly into a dry cup.

MEASURING LIQUID INGREDIENTS

Measure liquid ingredients in a liquid measuring cup; to read, set the cup on a flat surface and view the measurement at eye level.

TOASTING AND GRINDING NUTS

To toast nuts such as pecans, walnuts, and almonds, spread them on a baking sheet and cook in a 350°F oven until fragrant, about 10 minutes. (Start checking after 6 minutes if toasting sliced or chopped nuts.) Toast pine nuts at 350°F for 5 to 7 minutes. Toast hazelnuts in a 375°F oven until skins split, about 10 to 12 minutes; when cool enough to handle, rub warm nuts in a clean kitchen towel to remove skins. Chop cooled nuts coarsely or finely with a chef's knife, or pulse them in a food processor to grind. (Do not overprocess, or nuts will turn into a paste.)

TOASTING SEEDS

Preheat oven to 350°F. Spread seeds in a single layer on a rimmed baking sheet. Toast, stirring once, until golden, about 12 minutes Let cool completely.

TOASTING COCONUT

To toast coconut flakes, spread them out on a baking sheet and bake at 325°F, stirring once, until golden, about 5 minutes.

GRATING NUTMEG

Nutmeg has a nutty, spicy flavor that beautifully complements aromatic spices such as cinnamon and ginger. Grating fresh nutmeg results in a more complex, nuanced flavor (whole nutmeg also has a longer shelf life). Use a nutmeg grater or a rasp-style grater. If you would like to substitute pre-ground nutmeg for freshly grated, use about half the amount.

MELTING CHOCOLATE

Melt chopped chocolate in a metal bowl set over a pan of barely simmering water, or in a double-boiler. Alternatively, you can melt chocolate in the microwave: In a microwave-safe bowl, heat chocolate in 30-second intervals, stirring after each, until almost melted. Remove from microwave and stir to melt completely.

ZESTING CITRUS

Use a rasp-style grater such as a Microplane to remove citrus fruits' flavorful zest while leaving the bitter white pith behind. A citrus zester (a small tool with a row of small, sharp holes at one end) makes decorative curls for garnishes.

GRATING ZUCCHINI

Grate zucchini on the large holes of a box grater; squeeze dry in a clean kitchen towel.

INGREDIENTS

Flours and Grains

WHEAT FLOURS

The gluten in wheat flour gives rise, structure, lightness, and elasticity to breads and baked sweets. Whole-wheat flours are milled from the entire grain—bran, endosperm, and germ. Each type of flour brings different flavors and textures to baked goods. Many of these baked goods also rely on some all-purpose flour, which is milled so that little to none of the bran layer and germ remain. Generally, the all-purpose is used to balance the flavors of the whole-grain flours and the texture as well; it often helps to produce baked goods that are not overly dense or crumbly (as they can be when baked entirely from whole-grain flours).

WHOLE-WHEAT FLOUR
Most flour labeled as "whole wheat" is ground from hard red wheat, unless otherwise indicated. It has a pronounced, slightly bitter earthiness, and produces more richly flavored baked goods with a denser, coarser crumb and a chewier texture than those baked only with all-purpose flour. For baked goods with an airier crumb, it's best to combine whole-wheat flour with all-purpose flour or spelt flour; start by swapping half the all-purpose flour for whole-wheat, increasing the liquid gradually (a tablespoon at a time) if the dough or batter seems dry. We like whole-wheat in many yeasted bread recipes, as well as quick-breads and pie doughs.

GRAHAM FLOUR
Most commonly known for the namesake crackers, this flour is named for Sylvester Graham, a nineteenth-century minister who preached the value of whole grains. It is now the name given to coarsely ground whole-wheat flour, but the type of wheat can vary in terms of protein content and hardness and softness. Graham flour lends a robust honey flavor and rustic texture to baked goods and can require more liquid (add it a tablespoon at a time if the dough or batter seems dry) than other types of whole wheat.

OTHER WHEAT-RELATED FLOURS
Some ancient relatives of wheat, including Kamut (a trademarked name for golden, buttery flavored khorasan wheat); emmer (another name for farro, with flavors similar to spelt); and einkorn (the oldest variety, a small-berried type of farro that also tastes a bit like spelt) are becoming popular because of their lower gluten content and distinctive flavors. Flours from these increasingly available grains are worthy of experimentation. Try using them in place of whole-wheat or spelt flours in any recipe.

SPELT FLOUR
Spelt is an ancient, nonhybridized relative of wheat that has a sweet, spice-like flavor. It produces baked goods with a lighter, more tender crumb than those made with whole-wheat. Spelt is easier to digest for many people than wheat, but it is not gluten-free. It is a great first whole-grain flour to try because it

whole-wheat
pastry flour

whole-wheat
flour

farro
flour

graham
flour

sprouted
spelt
flour

white
whole-wheat
flour

spelt
flour

wheat
bran

wheat
germ

all-purpose
flour

coconut flour

almond flour

brown rice flour

oat flour

rolled oats

hazelnut flour

teff flour

chickpea flour

oat bran

cornmeal, fine

cornmeal, medium

rye flour

buckwheat flour

millet flour

millet

amaranth flour

quinoa flour

quinoa

barley flour

can be substituted one-to-one for all-purpose or whole-wheat flour in most recipes, as long as they don't require yeast. (You may need to increase the amount of liquid; use a tablespoon at a time if the dough or batter seems dry.)

WHEAT GERM AND WHEAT BRAN
Wheat germ and wheat bran are not whole grains; instead, they are the healthiest parts of the wheat berry. Wheat bran is ground from the fiber-filled outer layer of the berry, while wheat germ is ground from the ultra-nutritious, oil-rich center. Both can be used to boost the healthiness of baked goods and substituted for some of a recipe's all-purpose flour. Both wheat germ and wheat bran should be kept in the refrigerator or freezer to keep them from turning rancid. Toasted wheat germ is more flavorful than untoasted.

WHITE WHOLE-WHEAT FLOUR
Milled from hard white spring wheat, this whole-grain flour gives baked goods a milder flavor and slightly softer texture than traditional whole-wheat flour. It can be substituted for at least half of the all-purpose flour in a recipe, generally.

WHOLE-WHEAT PASTRY FLOUR
Like white pastry flour, whole-wheat pastry flour is lower in protein. The flour is milled from whole kernels of soft spring wheat, producing tender piecrusts, pastries, and some breads while still adding the nutritional benefits of a whole-grain flour. While the flour can be used by itself in pastry doughs, the resulting crusts usually aren't as flaky as those made with a 50/50 blend of all-purpose.

OTHER FLOURS AND GRAINS

Barley and rye are commonly associated with malt, which is used to make beer. As flours, they add distinctive flavors to baked goods. Since both have less gluten than wheat flours, they are usually blended with all-purpose or another wheat flour to give baked goods the right structure and lift.

BARLEY
Barley flour adds an intriguing flavor to biscuits, scones, cookies, cakes, and quickbreads. Extraordinarily fine, barley flour produces baked goods with a lovely, tender crumb and a caramelized, nutty flavor. Too high of a proportion of this flour may prevent baked goods from rising, however; when experimenting, try replacing one-third of all-purpose flour with barley flour.

RYE
Ground from cool-climate-loving rye berries, this flour comes in two versions: dark, which is usually whole grain, and a light variety that is sifted to remove some of the bran and germ, which helps create lighter baked goods. Rye flour smells surprisingly fruity; the sourness usually associated with it comes from the caraway seed often used to make rye bread. Breads made from 100 percent rye flour can be dense and a bit gummy. Rye flour's flavor is lovely in cookies and piecrusts. When experimenting, start by replacing half the wheat flour with rye; unlike with most whole-grain flours, you usually don't have to add more liquid.

About Chemical Leaveners

Baking soda and baking powder both lighten the texture of cakes, muffins, quickbreads, and the like. Baking soda needs an acidic ingredient, like buttermilk, yogurt, or apple cider, to be effective. Baking powder is simply baking soda mixed with an acid to help it work. Some brands of baking powder contain acids derived from aluminum and impart a slightly metallic taste to baked goods. If you want to avoid the metallic taste, seek out aluminum-free baking powder. If gluten is an issue for you, confirm that the label on your baking powder says "gluten free." Baking soda is naturally free of aluminum and gluten.

GLUTEN-FREE WHOLE-GRAIN FLOURS

Each of the following flours, and sometimes the whole grains themselves, brings their own flavors and textures to baked goods, but none of them can replace all-purpose flour in most recipes. All-purpose gluten-free flours are available; they are made from carefully calculated and often wildly different blends of grains, starches, and sometimes gums (like xanthan) that are designed to perform in combination like wheat flour. The ingredients in each blend, and thus the flavors and textures imparted, vary by brand. While we do not call for any gluten-free all-purpose flour in this book, you can substitute it for the regular all-purpose in these recipes; after testing many gluten-free blends, our test kitchen favorite is Cup4Cup brand. (www.cup4cup.com)

AMARANTH
Like quinoa, amaranth is another crop with South American roots. This protein-rich seed harvested from the amaranth shrub was the most important food in the ancient Aztec diet. It is now an important crop in many parts of the world, including China, Russia, and Thailand. This tiny pseudo-grain (about the size of a period at the end of a sentence) can be ground into flour or left whole to add a little crunch to granolas, pancakes, and other breakfast baked goods. Its grassy flavor can be strong, so start by swapping in one-sixth the amount of flour with amaranth flour. (That's ¼ cup for every 1½ cups of total flour used.) You can add a few tablespoons of the whole (not ground) grain to granolas and cookie doughs.

BROWN RICE
Brown rice flour, as well as regular rice flour, is commonly used in gluten-free cooking and baking, especially when a neutral-flavored flour is desired. Like other whole-grain flours, brown rice flour contains the hull and germ, while white rice flour has just the starch. Brown rice flour can make baked goods slightly heavier than white rice flour, but they are often interchangeable. Because baked goods made exclusively with the flour are gritty, the flour is best mixed with other flours. Swap out up to half of the other flours for rice flour.

BUCKWHEAT
Believe it or not, buckwheat has nothing to do with wheat; the name is believed to have originated because buckwheat resembles the seeds from a beech tree. Eventually "beech wheat" became "buckwheat." In truth, buckwheat is a seed from a plant that's related to rhubarb and is therefore classified as a pseudo-grain. Whether ground fine or coarse, this gluten-free flour has a dark grayish-brown color and powerful, distinctively earthy flavor. Buckwheat flour stands alone in some crepes, waffles, and blini recipes. More often, however, it's blended with wheat flour or other starches (start by swapping in one-third buckwheat flour) to add another flavor dimension to baked goods; it's especially tasty with dark chocolate and dried fruit.

CORNMEAL/CORN FLOUR

Inherently free of gluten, cornmeal is often blended with wheat flours (a one-to-one ratio is a good place to start) to give baked goods some structure. The grind of cornmeal can vary from so fine that it's called corn flour (used in cakes, pastry, or anywhere you don't want the grittiness), to fine (best for pancakes, muffins, and biscuits), to medium (great for cornbread), to coarse (best used for grits or any baked goods where a more rustic texture is desired). (Polenta, the Italian cornmeal porridge, is made with medium- or coarse-grind cornmeal.) To give baked goods a pronounced corn flavor (without too much grittiness), you can combine corn flour with cornmeal. For the most nutritious and flavorful cornmeal and corn flour, make sure the package says "whole grain" or "stone-ground"; this means that the germ and bran layer are included. Corn flour's flavor is especially good with fruit desserts, including anything made with citrus or summer fruits, like peaches or berries. Cornmeal also pairs well with cheese, chiles, and savory herbs. Replace up to one-half the amount of all-purpose flour with cornmeal or corn flour (or a mix of both).

MILLET

This tiny yellow seed has been around for many millennia and is still a dietary staple in parts of Africa, India, and China. While often used as birdseed in the United States, it is also becoming popular among home cooks there too, because of its gluten-free properties and mild, popcorn-like flavor. Whole millet can be cooked so it's fluffy (like couscous) or into a porridge (like oatmeal). When ground into flour, it can be used in baked goods with a delicate, cakelike crumb. Replace up to one-quarter of the wheat flour in baked goods with millet flour, or throw a few tablespoons of the whole seeds into granolas, muffins and quickbread batters, and cookie doughs. We like to add millet whole to cookies, muffins, and granolas for a pleasant crunch.

OAT BRAN

Like wheat bran, oat bran is milled from the oat's outer fiber-rich layer. Swap out one-quarter of the flour for oat bran to add concentrated amounts of fiber (there are 7 grams per ⅓ cup) to baked goods, including muffins and quickbreads.

OATS

Anyone who has ever had an oatmeal cookie knows that rolled oats give baked goods a pleasant chewiness. The flour, ground from whole-grain rolled oats, has a similar effect, with a mild, milky flavor that works well in muffins, cookies, pancakes, scones, sandwich breads, and biscuits. (It's actually the easiest flour to mill at home: Simply pulse the oats in a food processor until ground fine, and then sift.) When used in proportions that are too high, oat flour can make baked goods unappealingly gummy; using oat flour in place of about one-third all-purpose is a good place to start. While oats are indeed free of gluten, they are often processed in the same facilities as wheat. To be certain that oats or oat flour haven't been contaminated with gluten, be sure that the label says they're truly gluten free.

What Is Sprouted Flour?

Sprouted flour is made from grains and legumes that are exposed to heat and moisture just until they start to sprout; they are then dried before milling into flour. The process converts them from dormant seeds to living plants, increasing their nutritional value (sprouted grains have more vitamins B and C, for example). They're also easier to digest because their complex starches are converted to simpler vegetable sugars. Sprouted flours tend to have milder flavors than their basic whole-grain counterparts. When using sprouted flours, you usually need less liquid than you would for regular whole-grain flours. We found the most success using sprouted flour in recipes that don't rely on much gluten for structure, like the Sprouted Spelt Honey-Cashew Blondies on page 114.

QUINOA

This seed, another pseudo-grain, was once sacred to the ancient Incas and is now revered as a modern-day miracle food because of its high protein and fiber content. When the flour is added to baked goods, its pronounced flavor is almost sesame-like. When adding quinoa flour to baked goods, start by replacing one-quarter of the other flours with it, because its flavor is so assertive. Quinoa can also be cooked and added whole to pancakes and other simple batters.

TEFF

The tiniest grain is also one of the mightiest: In addition to its high fiber and protein content, it's rich with calcium. This chestnut-colored grain is the key ingredient in the sour Ethiopian flatbread called injera. When blended with all-purpose flour, teff's fine texture produces baked goods with a light crumb. Its rich malty flavor is terrific with roasted nuts and dried fruit, as wells as with chocolate. Because the flavor of teff is so strong, start by swapping out no more than one-quarter of the flour in a recipe for teff flour.

OTHER GLUTEN-FREE FLOURS

COCONUT FLOUR

A natural by-product of coconut milk production, this flour made from dried ground coconut has very little of the fat left from the coconut meat. With large amounts of fiber (5 grams for every 2 tablespoons) and a mild coconut flavor, it has become an important product for gluten-free bakers and those who follow low-carbohydrate diets. When coconut flour is used on its own, the resulting baked goods can be dense and dry, so it's best to blend it with other flours and add more eggs for moisture; start by swapping out no more than one-quarter of the amount of flour for coconut flour. For each ¼ cup coconut flour used, add an additional egg.

LEGUME FLOURS

Ground from dried beans, including chickpeas and soybeans, these gluten-free flours add protein and fiber to baked goods. For sweets, they're commonly found blended with other flours because they can impart a "beany" flavor; use no more than one-third bean flour in a dessert recipe. Savory baked goods can sometimes include more legume flour, like the Chickpea-Vegetable Pancakes on page 16, which are made exclusively with chickpea flour.

NUT FLOURS

Also called nut meals, nut flours are finely ground from untoasted nuts and can be used to enrich the flavor of baked goods (and boost the protein content, too). They can be blended with all-purpose flour or gluten-free flours. In some cakes (particularly tortes), nut flours can stand on their own in cakes. You can buy pre-ground nut flours, including almond, hazelnut, pecan, and walnut, but it's easy enough to make your own in a food processor or very powerful blender. See "More About Nut and Seed Flours" on the follwing page for instructions.

Grind Your Own Flours

Bakers who love working with whole grains and alternative flours might want to try grinding their own flours, which result in fresher, more flavorful, and less expensive ones than store-bought. Here are three methods for milling your own flour.

1. Manual mills: These inexpensive metal hand-crank mills attach to the kitchen counter; they're available from online retailers. Use them to grind grains, nuts, and seeds. They provide a serious arm workout to boot. (It takes about 2 minutes to grind 1 cup of flour.) While you can adjust the grind of the flour, it's hard to use this to make superfine flours without having to sift afterward.

2. High-powered blenders: Blenders that can reach over 20,000 rpm (rotations per minute) are strong enough to grind whole grains, as well as nuts and seeds for flour. (Vitamix and Blendtec are well-known brands.) The blender blades wear down over time and the jar can scratch, so it may be worth having a second jar just for making flour if you plan to do this often.

3. Electric grain mills: These mills grind large amounts of grains and legumes quickly, with little effort, and usually can create finer flours than a manual mill. The downside is that these mills cannot grind nuts or seeds and can cost between $150 and $400, so this option is best for those who are truly committed to grinding their own.

More About Nut and Seed Flours

To make nut and seed flours (also known as nut and seed meals), you can use a hand-crank mill or a high-powered blender, as described at left, but you can also use a standard food processor or blender. To prevent your nut flour from becoming nut butter, use nuts at room temperature and pulse rather than process continuously. It also helps to work with only 1 cup at a time. For extra insurance, add some of the flour or sugar from your recipe to help keep it powdery. To create an extra-fine nut flour, sift after grinding, or use a spice or coffee grinder for small amounts.

A KEY TO BAKING WITH WHOLE-GRAIN FLOURS

TYPE OF	HOW TO USE	FLAVOR PROFILE
Whole-wheat, regular or pastry	On its own or blended with all-purpose.	Brown sugar, lightly bitter and tannic.
White whole-wheat	On its own or blended with all-purpose.	Neutral.
Spelt	In place of all-purpose or whole-wheat, or blended with either.	Like whole-wheat flour without the bitterness.
Barley	Blended with all-purpose. Use no more than 50 percent.	Mild with a slight nutty sweetness.
Rye	Blended with all-purpose. In most cases, use no more than 50 percent.	Sweet and malty.
Amaranth	As a whole grain or blended with all-purpose or other flours; start by using no more than 15 percent in a flour blend.	Assertive, hay-like.
Brown rice	In gluten-free flour blends; use no more than 50 percent.	Neutral.
Buckwheat	On its own or blended with all-purpose or gluten-free flours.	Toasty, earthy, almost sour, like wine.
Corn	Blended with all-purpose or other gluten-free flours.	Buttery, tastes distinctly of sweet corn.
Millet	As a whole grain or blended with other flours; start by using no more than 25 percent.	Mild, popcorn-like.
Oats	Rolled or ground as a flour; start by using no more than 30 percent in a flour blend.	Milky and mild.
Quinoa	As a cooked whole grain or ground as a flour and blended with other flours; start by using no more than 25 percent.	Mildly sesame-like.
Teff	Blended with all-purpose or gluten-free blends; start by using no more than 20 percent.	Intensely malty.

BEST USES	FLAVOR PAIRINGS
Regular is best in breads, cookies, and breakfast baked goods; pastry flour is best for pie dough.	Brown sugar; maple; sweet spices; autumnal fruit; yeast.
Desserts or breads in which you don't want the flavor of the flour to overpower other ingredients.	Vanilla; lemon; summer fruits.
Any sweets and breads where you want a richer, sweeter flavor than all-purpose.	Bananas; butter; chocolate; stone fruits; sweet spices; almonds and cashews.
Sweet or savory batters or doughs that can benefit from a fine flour and don't require lots of gluten, like biscuits and some cakes.	Buttermilk; orange; berries; jam.
Baked sweets and breads that can benefit from its hearty texture and flavor.	Walnuts, pecans, and hazelnuts; sweet spices; chocolate; tangy fruits like rhubarb; yeast.
As a whole grain in granolas and cookies; as a flour in baked goods like coffee cake that would benefit from its flavor.	Molasses; brown sugar; orange; honey; sweet spices.
As a base flour in gluten-free baked goods such as sandwich bread.	Vanilla; brown sugar.
Baked goods (gluten-free or not) that can stand up to its intense flavor.	Chocolate; dark spice, molasses; honey; dried fruit; walnuts, pecans, and hazelnuts.
Baked goods that can benefit from its sweet flavor, like cookies, muffins, and quickbreads.	Butter; cheese; herbs; lemon; peaches; berries; citrus.
As a whole grain in cookies, granolas, breads, and muffins for a pleasing crunch; as a flour in gluten-free sweets like muffins and pancakes that would benefit from its gentle sweetness.	Butter; honey; cooked squash; vanilla.
Use rolled oats in cookies, muffins, quickbreads, or toppings for fruit desserts. As a flour, add to bread, muffins, and cookies.	Butter; berries; brown sugar; maple.
Baked goods such as pastry and pie dough (gluten-free or not) that can benefit from its pronounced flavor.	Orange; molasses; honey; dates.
Baked goods such as quickbread (gluten-free or not) that can benefit from its pronounced flavor.	Browned butter; hazelnuts; dried fruit; honey; molasses; yeast.

Fats

Fat is essential to the flavor and texture of nearly all baked goods. For the best-tasting results, we encourage you to buy the best-quality oils, butter, and other fats you can, and be sure they smell fresh—never rancid—before using.

COCONUT OIL

Coconut oil is often used as a butter substitute in vegan or dairy-free baking because it is solid up to 76°F. Virgin coconut oil, which is unrefined, imparts a sweet, fragrant flavor to baked goods, and is especially tasty in baked goods made with chocolate. Look for it sold in jars, and be sure it says "virgin," "extra-virgin," or "unrefined" on the label; otherwise, it's refined and flavorless.

NEUTRAL OILS

Oils such as safflower and sunflower are great for imparting moisture to muffins and quickbreads without overpowering their flavors. These oils also trim the amount of saturated fat in baked goods, if that is a concern. For the healthiest version of these neutral oils, look for "organic" as well as "high oleic," which means they are higher in monounsaturated fats.

NUT AND SEED BUTTERS

Ground nuts and ground seeds can sometimes be used in place of flour, but when processed until they form a paste, or butter, they can be substituted for some or all of the butter in a recipe. Depending on the nut, the butters impart different flavors. You can buy a large variety of freshly ground nut butters at many health food stores or make your own using the instructions on page 282.

OLIVE OIL

Rich with monounsaturated fats, olive oil, particularly extra-virgin olive oil, is one fat that is universally admired; it's consistently shown to be especially good for you. Extra-virgin olive oil is from the first pressing of the olives, which produces a higher quality oil than pure olive oil; it also has a strong concentration of health-promoting polyphenols. For baking, we prefer a mild-flavored, everyday quality oil and like to pair it with citrus, cornmeal, and dried fruit.

UNSALTED BUTTER

Baking with butter creates incomparably flaky, golden crusts and rich-tasting cookies and cakes. We prefer using unsalted butter so we can control how much salt is in a recipe (and because it tends to be fresher). For the best flavor, seek out organic butter from grass-fed (also known as pastured) cows, which contains more heart-healthy omega-3 fatty acids than butter from grain-fed cows.

unsalted
butter

safflower
oil

virgin
coconut
oil

almond
butter

peanut
butter

extra-
virgin
olive oil

Greek yogurt

almond milk

buttermilk

milk

coconut milk

plain yogurt

Dairy Products (and Alternatives)

Dairy products add moisture and some fat to baked goods; cultured dairy products, like buttermilk and yogurt, make baked goods especially tender. In many cases, vegan alternatives, like nut milks and coconut milk, can be substituted for the milk or cream in recipes.

BUTTERMILK

Traditional buttermilk is actually a by-product of butter making and has become more widely available at farmers' markets. If you can find it, snatch it up; it will impart an incredible flavor to your baked goods. Supermarket buttermilk has actually been inoculated with a culture and is not quite the same; it works just fine in baking recipes however. If you are out of buttermilk, it's easy to make your own. See page 281 for details.

COCONUT MILK

Full-fat coconut milk, which is usually sold in cans, is a good substitute for heavy cream in many recipes, such as the Chocolate-Coconut Pie on page 145. (You can also make your own; see page 283.) The coconut milk that's sold in cartons in the refrigerator section of the grocery store is watered down, so it's quite low in fat and is a good substitute for recipes that call for dairy milk or almond milk.

MILK

Whole milk is less processed than low-fat and nonfat (skim) milks, which is why we prefer it for the recipes in this book. Plus, the extra fat gives the baked goods more flavor and moisture.

NUT MILKS

Made from soaked, pureed, and strained nuts, these milks have become a popular substitute for soy and rice milks, as well as for dairy products. Homemade versions (see instructions on page 282) are more flavorful than store bought, most of which contain stabilizing agents. However, when baking, either type works well.

TOFU

Made from coagulated soy milk, tofu can be used in place of eggs in custards to make vegan recipes. When baking, opt for soft silken versions of tofu, which are easy to blend into batters.

YOGURT

Unless otherwise specified, use plain, full-fat yogurt for the recipes in this book or use homemade (page 284). Some recipes may call for Greek yogurt, which is strained yogurt that is thick like whipped cream and works well in cheesecakes and cream pies. It's also a delicious, less sweet substitute for ice cream as an accompaniment to chocolate cakes and fruit desserts.

muscovado
sugar

dates

confectioners'
sugar

turbinado
sugar

natural
cane

granulated
sugar

molasses

maple
syrup

coconut

honey

Sweeteners

Granulated sugar is the standard sweetener for most baking recipes. We like working with less processed versions of cane sugar, however, as well as alternative natural sugars, like coconut sugar, to add different dimensions of flavor to baked goods.

CANE SUGARS

CONFECTIONERS' SUGAR
This sugar is essentially just sugar that's ground fine and blended with starch to create a light powder. (To make your own; see page 280.)

MUSCOVADO SUGAR
Commercial brown sugar is made from refined granulated sugar that's later mixed with molasses. Muscovado is its unprocessed cousin: it's sugarcane juice that's simply boiled until crystals form so it's never separated from the molasses (this way, it's still moist and sticky). It also retains some of sugarcane's natural nutrients, including calcium, iron, magnesium, and many vitamins. Use it one-for-one in place of light or dark brown sugar, packing it into measuring cups as you would brown sugar.

NATURAL CANE SUGAR
Sometimes sold as evaporated cane juice or organic sugar, these pale blond granules are a less refined substitute for more commonly available white granulated sugar. We like that it has a slightly richer flavor than white sugar and is often farmed organically. It also tends to be vegan, meaning it was not refined with any animal by-products (including charcoal made from cow bones), as some white sugar is. You can replace this cup-for-cup in any recipes that calls for granulated sugar. Because the grains are slightly coarser and moister, the texture of the baked goods can change slightly. Superfine sugar is often used for recipes in which you want the sugar to dissolve, like whipped cream or meringue. You can grind natural cane sugar until fine in a food processor. Keep in mind, however, that the color will be affected slightly; meringues and buttercream icings, for example, will not be as white when made with cane sugar as with superfine.

TURBINADO/DEMERARA SUGAR
Amber-hued and less refined than evaporated cane juice, this is often called "raw sugar," or demerara; one well-known brand is Sugar in the Raw. It has a gentle molasses flavor and coarse, crunchy texture that's terrific for sprinkling on all kinds of baked goods before baking.

UNSULFURED MOLASSES
This thick, sticky syrup is the by-product created when sugar is refined. It contains many nutrients, including iron, vitamin B_6, calcium, and magnesium. Unless a recipe says otherwise, avoid the most intense grade of molasses, known as blackstrap, which can make baked goods taste bitter.

About Salt

Salt is crucial in most baked goods recipes—it helps bring out the sweetness as well as other flavors. Most of the recipes in this book call for coarse salt, which includes kosher salts. If you want to substitute fine table or sea salt, reduce the amount slightly (by ¼ teaspoon for every 1¼ teaspoons coarse salt called for).

OTHER NATURAL SWEETENERS

COCONUT SUGAR

Derived from the sap of flower buds of the coconut palm tree, this sugar has no coconut flavor. Instead, it's caramel-like and not overly sweet; in fact, it has almost complex notes. It works best in moist baked goods that include other sweeteners, like the banana-and-pineapple sweetened Hummingbird Cake on page 204.

DATES

Soaked and blended to a paste, dates are a terrific natural sweetener. They add tons of fiber and vitamins to baked goods. We especially love date paste in the Fruit and Honey Nut Bars on page 123.

HONEY

Sweeter than sugar, honey is a fragrant sweetener that comes in many, many different varieties, each of which has its own distinctive flavor. Once thought to be food of the gods, honey has been used as a folk remedy for thousands of years, and for good reason—the golden nectar is loaded with health-promoting enzymes, minerals, prebiotics (which help feed bacteria), and antioxidants. Choose raw honey over processed, as the high heat used during processing can destroy many of the beneficial compounds. You can replace sugar with honey in simple baking recipes, like muffins and quickbreads; use ¾ cup honey for every cup of sugar, and reduce the liquid in the recipe by ¼ cup for every cup of honey used. You should also reduce the oven temperature by 25°F because honey can cause baked goods to darken faster.

MAPLE SYRUP

Made from the boiled sap of sugar maple trees, this syrup has a rich flavor that's perfect in granolas and muffins. Syrup labeled as "Grade B" or "Dark with Robust Taste" is often the tastiest in baked goods, but any pure maple syrup works well. When replacing sugar with maple syrup, follow the same rules as you would for honey (see above).

OTHER FRUITS

Applesauce and mashed bananas can act as sweeteners in baked goods while also adding moisture (so you can use less fat). If you want to make healthier simple baked goods, including muffins, pancakes, and quickbreads, start by replacing half the fat with the same amount of applesauce or mashed banana, then reduce the sugar by one-quarter.

Seeds

Replete with healthy fats, seeds add not only moisture and density but also a satisfying crunch and distinctive flavors—further enhanced by toasting or grinding—to baked goods. They're also a great substitute for nuts when baking for people with allergies. The richness of seeds, bursting as they are with flavor and nutrition, is not surprising when you consider that each little capsule is essentially a plant's embryo, containing everything needed to begin life (given the right temperature and water). Many of these little pods have been hailed as superfoods, packed with vitamins, minerals, fiber, antioxidants, and beneficial fatty acids. Their oil content makes them especially perishable, so buy yours at a grocer where turnover is high, and store them in resealable bags, preferably in the freezer.

ANISE

The distinctive licorice flavor of this seed is used in sweets and liqueurs worldwide—including Italian anisette cookies and spirits like Greek ouzo and Middle Eastern arak. It is often confused with the similar-tasting fennel, but anise seeds are smaller and their flavor is more concentrated and floral.

BLACK AND WHITE SESAME

The mildly sweet sesame was one of the first oilseed crops to be domesticated. Now it can be found in almost every cuisine, from Japanese to Middle Eastern to Indian. The difference between the two varieties is largely aesthetic, as they taste quite similar.

BROWN AND GOLDEN FLAX

This suddenly ubiquitous seed achieved superfood status when studies showed it may protect against many illnesses, including cancer and heart disease. The health benefits of flaxseeds are more easily absorbed when they are consumed ground rather than whole. Freshly ground seeds work better (and taste fresher) than pre-ground seeds. Flaxseed can replace eggs in vegan baked goods because they become gel-like when soaked. For each egg you would like to substitute, soak 1 tablespoon ground seeds in 3 tablespoons water for 10 minutes.

CARAWAY

The fragrant caraway seed is a prominent ingredient in eastern European and Scandinavian baked goods, including rye breads.

CHIA

These tiny seeds are a true superfood: They're rich in omega-3 fatty acids, fiber, and antioxidants. Like flax, they form a gel when soaked that thickens batters and can be used as an egg substitute in simple baked goods, like muffins and quickbreads. (A good rule of thumb: For 1 large egg, soak 1 tablespoon ground chia seeds in 3 tablespoons water for 5 minutes.)

CUMIN

Cumin, which adds an earthy flavor and medium spiciness to Indian, Middle Eastern, and South American cuisines, is often used in its ground form. (For the freshest flavor, toast and grind your own seeds.) In traditional medicine, cumin has long been used as a digestive aid.

FENNEL

A common ingredient in Chinese five-spice powder, Italian sausage, and many Indian curries, fennel is revered for its aromatic pungency and its digestive benefits. Puritans called it the "meeting seed" because, according to some historians, it was thought to fend off hunger during long sermons.

HEMP

Seeds from the hemp plant—the stalks of which were long harvested for nonfood uses like clothing and rope—are newly celebrated for their high levels of essential fatty acids, protein, and antioxidants. It is part of the cannabis family, but is not to be confused with what is cultivated as marijuana.

NIGELLA

Tiny, stark black nigella seeds, which have a nutty, peppery flavor, are often used in Indian spice mixes and as a topping for breads such as naan.

POPPY

Once considered a natural sleep aid (not surprising, since the poppy plant also yields opium), the dusky seeds are common toppings for breads and bagels. When ground, they gain flavor and intensity, providing a rich base for the sweet paste that is a popular filling in eastern European baked goods such as strudel and hamantaschen.

PUMPKIN

In culinary terminology, these are often called pepitas, their Spanish name, especially when they have been hulled to reveal the green interiors. These protein- and antioxidant-rich seeds work well in breads and granolas, but they also make a great snack when roasted and salted.

SUNFLOWER

Often consumed on their own as a snack, the hulled sunflower "seeds" are more accurately called the kernels or hearts. Nutlike and substantial, they are also a popular source of cooking oil and sunflower butter, an allergen-free alternative to peanut butter.

black and white
sesame

fennel

cumin

hemp

sunflower

poppy

anise

caraway

nigella

brown and
golden flax

pumpkin

ACKNOWLEDGMENTS

All of us at Martha Stewart Living love to bake, and we've been baking cakes, cupcakes, pies, cookies, tarts, biscuits, and breads for many years. And as much as we have our longtime favorites, in the past few years we've found ourselves tweaking many recipes, experimenting with newly available and intriguing flours, fats, and sweeteners. Along the way, we've made all kinds of delicious discoveries. Chief among our experimenters is MSL food editor Shira Bocar. She is the mastermind behind this project, and we are grateful for the careful consideration she put into it—creating delicious original recipes, testing to get everything just right, and lending her food-styling skills to the photographs. She was joined in her development and styling efforts by the talented team of Jason Schreiber and Samantha Seneviratne, and all were ably assisted by Caitlin Brown, Nicole Coppola, Denise Ginley, Josefa Palacios, and Gertrude Porter. Other recipes, as well as invaluable guidance, were offered by Jennifer Aaronson, Sarah Carey, Anna Kovel, Greg Lofts, Lucinda Scala Quinn, Laura Rege, and Lauryn Tyrell.

Editorial director Ellen Morrissey and managing editor Susanne Ruppert oversee the production of all of our books, from start to finish. For this project, they were joined by editor and writer Kristin Donnelly, who cheerfully jumped on board and helped keep everything on track, organizing the recipes, tips, and information into one cohesive, practical volume. The team was also assisted by Ava Pollack and Christopher Rudolph.

Jennifer Wagner created the timeless, beautiful design and directed the new photography by our longtime friend, the exquisitely talented Jonathan Lovekin. Scot Schy lent his keen art direction to the photography shoots as well. A list of the other photographers whose work graces these pages can be found on page 4. Ayesha Patel styled the lovely props, assisted by Sarah Vasil. Denise Clappi and Spyridon Ginis helped ensure the quality of the gorgeous images. We are grateful as well to many others who helped out on this project, including Andie Diemer, John Myers, and Alison Vanek Devine.

And as always, we thank our publishing partners at Clarkson Potter, namely Jana Branson, Amy Boorstein, Doris Cooper, Debbie Glasserman, Carly Gorga, Linnea Knollmueller, Maya Mavjee, Mark McCauslin, Ashley Phillips Meyer, Marysarah Quinn, Kate Tyler, and Aaron Wehner.

RECIPES BY DIETARY PREFERENCE

Dairy-Free

Almond-Milk Custard Tart
Cherry-Date Oat Bars
Chocolate-Coconut Pie
Coconut Baked Oatmeal
Coconut-Pistachio Biscotti
Coconut-Pumpkin Bread Pudding
Fruit and Honey Nut Bars
Gluten-Free Sandwich Bread
Mixed-Seed Clusters
No-Knead Seeded Bread
Oat-and-Millet Granola
Seeded Graham Biscotti
Strawberry-Cherry
   Whole-Grain Crumble
Stuffed Whole-Wheat Flatbreads
Vegan Apple Pie
Vegan Banana-Oat Pancakes
Vegan French Toast
Vegan German Chocolate Cake
Vegan Lemon-Coconut Squares
Whole-Grain Seeded Wafer
   Crackers
Whole-Wheat Pita Bread

Gluten-Free

Almond-Coconut Macaroons
Cashew Butter and Jam
   Thumbprints
Chickpea-Vegetable Pancakes
Chocolate Buckwheat Torte
Coconut-Pistachio Financiers
Flourless Chocolate-Walnut Torte
Flourless Double-Chocolate Pecan
   Cookies
Gluten-Free Fudgy Pecan
   Brownies
Gluten-Free Sandwich Bread
Gluten-Free Quinoa Pancakes
Lemon-Cornmeal Cake
Spiced Pumpkin Pie with Crisp
   Rice Crust
Zucchini-Almond Cake

Nut-Free

Apple-Cider Doughnut Cake
Berry Cobbler with Cornmeal
   Biscuits
Blackberry-Oat Muffins
Blueberry Muffins
Buckwheat Espresso Cookies
Buckwheat Waffles with Fresh
   Ricotta and Citrus
Buttermilk Barley Biscuit
Parsnip-Rosemary Muffins
Chickpea-Vegetable Pancakes
Chocolate Beet Cake
Chocolate-Coconut Pie
Cinnamon-Apple Cranberry
   Crunch
Coconut Baked Oatmeal
Coconut-Pumpkin Bread Pudding
Corn Muffins
Cornmeal Drop Biscuits
Dark Chocolate-Spelt Brownies
Double Apple-Bran Muffins
Double Chocolate Rye Muffins
Gingerbread-Pumpkin Cakes
Gluten-Free Quinoa Pancakes
Graham Crackers
Graham-Flour and Jam Pastry
   Squares
Granola Cookies
Half-Moon Cookies
Herb Quiche with Rye Crust
Honey-Wheat Parker House Roll
Honey Whole-Wheat Bread
Irish-Style Brown Bread
Lattice-Topped Nectarine Pie
Lemon-Yogurt Cupcakes
Mixed-Berry Hand Pies
Molasses-Oat Bread
No-Knead Seeded Bread
Oat-and-Millet Granola
Oat Roulade with Berry-Cream
Oatmeal Shortbread
Orange-Barley Pound Cake
Pear Galette with Graham Crust

Pear-Oat Crisp
Pumpkin Spelt Scones with Maple
   Glaze
Rye Soft Pretzels
Sausage and Swiss Chard Strata
Seed and Whole-Grain Crackers
Seeded English Muffins
Seeded Saratoga Torte
Seeded Savory Quickbread
Soda Bread with Currants and
   Caraway
Spelt Butter Layer Cake with
   Whipped Cream and Berries
Spiced Apple and Oat Scones
Strawberry-Cherry Whole-Grain
   Crumble
Stuffed Whole-Wheat Flatbread
Sweet Potato-Cheesecake
   Squares
Vegan Apple Pie
Whole-Wheat Snickerdoodle Bites
Whole-Grain Cornbread
Whole-Grain Pumpkin Bread
Whole-Wheat Fig Crumble
   Squares
Whole-Wheat Monkey Bread
Whole-Wheat Pancakes
Whole-Wheat Pita Bread
Whole-Wheat Popovers
Whole-Wheat Snickerdoodle Bites

Vegan

Oat-and-Millet Granola
Vegan Apple Pie
Vegan Banana-Oat Pancakes
Vegan French Toast
Vegan German Chocolate Cake
Vegan Lemon-Coconut Squares
Whole-Grain Seeded Wafer
   Crackers
Stuffed Whole-Wheat Flatbreads

INDEX

Note: Page references in *italics* indicate photographs.